© 2011 MarriageKeepers Ministries, Inc. All rights reserved.

No part of this book may be reproduced, stored in a retrieval system, or transmitted by any means without the written permission the author.

First published by MarriageKeepers Ministries 02/20/2011

978-0-9833205-3-1 (sc)

Printed in the United States of America

Certain stock imagery @ iStockphoto, Bigstockphoto and Clipart.com.

Cover design and layout by Tony Barmann, saul2pauldesign.org.

Because of the dynamic nature of the Internet, any Web addresses or links contained in this book may have changed since publication and may no longer be valid.

renewed

A 30-day devotional challenge for husbands

Rob Thorpe

TABLE OF CONTENTS

Introduction .... Pages 7-8

Challenge Instructions .... Pages 9-10

Part 1 (Days 1-7) .... Pages 11-36

Part 2 (Days 8-14) .... Pages 37-64

Part 3 (Days 15-21) .... Pages 65-89

Part 4 (Days 22-30) .... Pages 90-123

Introduction – being a good husband is hard

There is no on ramp, no practice game, no apprenticeship for this. You go from being completely self-centered and single, to being completely self-centered and married. It has been said, "You don't realize just how selfish you really are until you get married."

Not much in life can adequately prepare you for being a husband. I'm talking about a good husband. Anyone can technically "be" a husband, but I'm assuming you are reading this because you are either a good husband wanting to get even better, or a struggling husband trying to become good. Either way, I applaud you. You have taken a huge step by reading <u>Husband - A User's Guide</u> and entering into this devotional challenge.

Most of us grew up without a role model for what a great husband looks like, and even those who did will admit, that having a great role model at home doesn't guarantee that you will be the same caliber husband to your wife. We are simply left to figure it out on our own - on the job training at its worst. The portrayals of husbands on television and movies don't provide any help, and the ones we get to observe first-hand seem to have the same issues and hang-ups we have. So, at the end of the day, we simply go home and "wing it". We try and do the best we can with what we know. And besides, our marriage isn't that bad. We're doing okay – right?

Trial and error is a great way to learn some things in this life. Discovering mom was right after all when she said the stove was hot, or that the cat will indeed scratch you if you squeezed him too hard. But trial and error is a very painful way to learn about marriage. There is way too much heartache, pain and scarring left behind.

The goal over the next thirty days is not to give you more information. Bookstores are full of good marriage information. Our goal is for you to become a more deliberate husband, and to listen to the voice of God every day. If you are willing, He will truly change your heart, and after thirty days (or even before) you will begin to witness real transformation in your life and in your marriage. Many of you will also find you will make greater progress if you complete this challenge with another man, or a small group of men. Men naturally resist it, but accountability is a great tool for change.

The most rewarding things this life has to offer come with a price, and many times you don't <u>feel</u> <u>like</u> paying that price to enjoy them.

- Obtaining a quality education
- Achieving success at work
- Staying physically fit & healthy
- Raising well-adjusted, obedient, loving children
- Enjoying a fulfilling, successful marriage
- Enjoying a comfortable, fruitful retirement

None of these successes will happen by themselves. You can't just sit back, do nothing, and enjoy the results. They all take time, hard work, and sacrifice – But, if you do work at them, you will love the results. Are you willing to pay the price to "win the race" as a husband?

Let's get started...

Challenge Instructions

Reading a book on marriage won't change your life. Filling in blanks for thirty days won't change your life. But - I am convinced that God can, and will, change your life, and your marriage, if you sincerely desire it and work through this Challenge with Him.

The Challenge is designed to facilitate life change by combining four crucial elements:

1. Spending extended time alone with God, asking Him to speak to you & recording what you hear.
2. Reading, and spending time thinking about (meditating on) God's Word, the Bible.
3. Conversing with God through prayer and humbly asking Him for real and lasting transformation.
4. Following through with any Action Steps and Exercises.

How do I know these elements will change your life?

> ➢ Throughout history spending time in God's presence has produced dramatic life change in people.
> See Moses in Exodus Chapter 3, and what happens in his life afterward. (see also Ex.33:11, and Gideon in Judges 6:22). Jesus said he could do nothing on his own, but only what the Father did (John 14:10). Jesus made time to get alone with the Father, (see Mark 1:35). God has always spoken to His people and continues to speak everyday, through His Word and by His Spirit into your spirit – if you quiet the noise in your life so you can hear Him.

> ➢ The Bible is not a book of stories made up by men, but the actual voice and wisdom of God. It is the only book in history that the Author comes with it. See Romans 3:2, and I Thessalonians 2:13. The words of the Bible are truth, and the truth will set you free from the things that bind you and hold you down. See John 17:17, and John 8:32. The Bible is a lamp unto your feet and a light unto

your path (showing you where to go in life). See Psalm 199:105. Approach your time in the Bible as a conversation starter with God. He longs to speak to you and give you the wisdom and direction you need. Openly talk with Him about what you are reading and listen closely as He speaks personally with you.

➤ Prayer changes things. We are told in Scripture that "we have not, because we ask not". (James 4:2) God is always listening and always attentive to your prayers. He may not always answer them the way you want, or in your time frame, but He always answers. Remember – prayer is a dialogue, not a monologue. God wants to commune, fellowship, interact with you – not just hear your "bless me" and "give me" lists. He is not your divine Santa Claus, or genie in a bottle that you summon only when you need something. He is a Father who loves you completely, and longs to abundantly bless you. He is sovereign and is always good.

Daily Instructions

Find a quiet place, away from all distractions, and expect God to meet with you and speak to you. Don't hurry through this. The goal is not to rush through the questions and write something in the blanks. The goal is to meet with God and actual hear what He is speaking.

Read the Scriptures for that day. Read them again. Ask God what He wants to say to you personally through His Word, and read them again. Read through the lesson, looking for personal application in your life and marriage. Listen for God to speak to you.

Pray the Crafted Prayer out loud, and pray anything else He puts on your heart to pray.

Sit quietly with God, pen in hand, and ask Him to speak to you as you write down thoughts and impressions from the day's lesson; be prepared to do what He leads you to do, even if you don't understand it or feel like it.

DAY 1

Colossians 1:16-17 - *For by him all things were created: things in heaven and on earth, visible and invisible, whether thrones or powers or rulers or authorities; all things were created by him and for him. He is before all things, and in him all things hold together.*

According to this verse, ALL THINGS are created by Him and for Him, and He is the one who holds everything together. So, it is fair to say that you and your wife were created by Him, for Him and are held together by Him. Your marriage was created by Him, and For Him, and He is the One who holds it together – if you allow Him.

You probably acknowledge that God created you, but you must also see that you are created FOR Him. Individually you are created to glorify God. As a married couple, your primary mission is to glorify God. How's that going so far?

In what ways would you say your marriage is glorifying God?
If not, why? _____
_____
_____

If you really grasped this truth, and woke every morning with the intent to glorify God in and through your marriage – how would your relationship with your wife change? _____
_____
_____

If you stop to think about it, you would most likely agree that God holds you together. You can't make your own heart beat. You can take vitamins, exercise and stop smoking – but it is God Who holds your life in His hands. Every breath, every heartbeat – is a gift from Him.

In the same way your marriage is held together by God. You didn't make your wife fall in love with you – God did. You don't have the power, patience and strength to live with the same woman for a lifetime – but God does. You were never meant to learn enough information or acquire enough essential skills to sustain a fulfilling, God-glorifying marriage. God designed husbands and wives to enjoy marriage – with Him. (See Genesis 2 &3). Marriage was, and is, to be lived out in the presence of the Creator – with His direct and loving involvement.

Right now, are you trying to "make your marriage work?" Are you trying to do things around the house to score brownie points with your wife, or have you stopped trying because nothing seems to be working?

> **As God by creation made two of one,**
> **so again by marriage He made one of two.**
> **~Thomas Adams**

Here is a simple, yet profound verse that directly applies to our role as husbands:

> *Matthew 4:18-20* - *As Jesus was walking beside the Sea of Galilee, he saw two brothers, Simon called Peter and his brother Andrew. They were casting a net into the lake, for they were fishermen. "Come, follow me," Jesus said, "and I will make you fishers of men." At once they left their nets and followed him.*

Jesus makes a simple promise to these rough fishermen – if you will follow me, "I WILL MAKE YOU fishers of men." He did not ask them to make themselves fishers of men, even though they knew a lot about fishing. He did not require that they clean up their past mistakes, or improve themselves or learn the Bible before they were worthy. All He asked was for them to "follow". The rest would be up to him.

That is what Jesus is asking of you as well. Jesus is asking you to follow Him first and foremost – and He will make you a "husband". Your response can either be to reject His invitation, or do what the fishermen did – "at once they left their nets and followed Him" Are you willing to give up your "best practices" and simply follow Him – every day? Your answer will be the primary determinate in whether you experience success in completing this Challenge, and your success in your marriage.

What would a day of following Jesus look like for you? _____
_____
_____
_____

Crafted Prayer

Father, I must confess that I continue to try and make my marriage better in my own strength. I realize that marriage was never intended to be lived apart from Your direct involvement. Forgive me for thinking I can do a better job than You. Would You show me how to be the best husband I can be to my wife? She deserves it, but I also want to bring You glory in my marriage. I want others to look at our marriage and see the love You have for Your bride, the church.

Today Lord, show me how to let go and trust You to make me the husband I was created to

> *"You are worthy, our Lord and God, to receive glory and honor and power, for you created all things, and by your will they were created and have their being."*
> *~ Revelation 4:11*

be. I want You to lead, and I want to follow. Please speak to me today, and lead me. Like the disciples, I let go of my know-how, and my best efforts, and simply trust You to lead us to a better place. Thank You that You are a God of fresh starts. I want to start fresh with You today, and with my wife today. Speak to me now as I quiet myself to listen to Your voice. I need to hear from You.

Notes: *What do you hear God saying to you concerning His responsibility to lead you and your marriage?* _____
_____
_____
_____
_____
_____
_____
_____

DAY 2

Genesis 2:18 - The Lord God said, "It is not good for the man to be alone. I will make a helper suitable for him."

As we saw yesterday, we are created by God and for His glory. The first man, Adam, was created by God and taken to a beautiful garden environment called Eden. The Bible doesn't tell us how long he was there alone, but I am convinced it was quite a while. Naming hundreds of thousands of animals would have taken a very long time. Adam wasn't actually alone, that is, in the sense that alone means "all by himself". Adam had a relationship with God, had meaningful work to do and had a multitude of animals around him. But God knew that Adam did not have anyone "like" him to share life with. After a while, Adam also knew.

It is so interesting that God created man with an "aloneness" that even He cannot (or does not) fill. God said that this aloneness is not good for us, and He carefully, purposefully designed a creature that would be Adam's perfectly suitable "helper". This word "helper" is used in the New Testament by Jesus when describing the Holy Spirit to his disciples. It describes an "essential helper" whose role is to offer assistance, comfort, support, relief, encouragement, and guidance.

We each have a God-designed need for someone "suitable" for us. Do you find it difficult to view your wife as this special gift from God? _____

How would your relationship with your wife change if you really did accept her in this way? _____
_____
_____
_____
_____
_____

God didn't just do this for Adam. He did it for you. The wife you are living with today was specifically, uniquely, purposefully designed (fashioned) by a loving Father – just for you. She, out of all the women on the planet, is uniquely qualified to complete you. It doesn't feel like it sometimes, but it's true. The sooner you begin to accept and appreciate (1) God – for giving you such a wonderful gift, and (2) your wife – for being that gift – even though she isn't perfect at it – the better your relationship will be.

When is the last time you thanked God for bringing you and your wife together? When is the last time you thanked your wife for being such a wonderful wife?

Action Step: Tell your wife one thing you appreciate about her today.

Your goal as a husband is to be the best you can be – not to change your wife or try to make her better. God will take care of that. What you need to concentrate on is yourself. One thing you need to do, and do often, is openly thank God for your wife. You should regularly express your thankfulness, take time to remember what attracted you to her and what you appreciate most about her. As you practice this, the little issues of marriage will begin to fade into obscurity.

Give thanks to the LORD, for he is good ~Psalm 107:1

List 5 things you like most about your wife – and why. These are **not** things like – she cooks my food, or buys groceries. Think of her heart, character and spiritual gifts.

1. _____
   _____
2. _____
   _____

3. _____
   _____

4. _____
   _____

5. _____
   _____

Crafted Prayer

Father, thank You for _____ (her name). I know I don't always appreciate her the way I should, but I want You to know I appreciate You creating her and bringing her to me. My life would be different, and incomplete without her.

Thank You for her character, and her spirit. Even though I don't see her the way You see her, I honestly want to do a better job of embracing her as Your perfect helper and completer. Forgive me for taking her for granted, and for not being more thankful for her.

Would you help me show her, in practical ways, how much she means to me and how thankful I am for her? I know she needs to hear that, and especially see that. Show me how to demonstrate my love to her. Give me the words to vocalize my feelings of love and appreciation for all she is, and for what she does. I want her to know I appreciate her.

Help me Lord to see _____ through Your eyes, and to openly appreciate her more often.

> *Her husband praises her: "There are many virtuous and capable women in the world, but you surpass them all!" Charm is deceptive, and beauty does not last; but a woman who fears the Lord will be greatly praised. Reward her for all she has done. Let her deeds publicly declare her praise.*
> *~ Proverbs 31: 28-31*

Notes: *What did you hear God saying about His creating an essential partner just for you?*

DAY 3

Genesis 2:21-2 - *So the Lord God caused the man to fall into a deep sleep; and while he was sleeping, he took one of the man's ribs and closed up the place with flesh. Then the Lord God made a woman from the rib he had taken out of the man, and he brought her to the man. The man said, "This is now bone of my bones and flesh of my flesh; she shall be called 'woman, for she was taken out of man."*

It is very interesting to note that Adam not only enjoyed a perfect external environment, but he also, more than any human ever, enjoyed a moment-by-moment fellowship with God Himself. He literally walked and talked with God all day long.

Yet, there was still something missing in Adam's heart and soul. Something that not even his relationship with God could fill. Somehow God created a personal need, void, longing in the heart of man that can only be met through an earthly relationship with his wife. Eve was not just a fellow human or a close female friend. Genesis 2:22 clearly indicates more than just a personal introduction – this was Adam and Eve's marriage (evidenced by the words "wife" and "husband" from this point onward).

Adam was obviously ecstatic. He was no longer single! Finally, there was another creature "like" himself. The verb tense in Scripture tells us that Adam literally shouted. He exclaimed, "Finally, – THIS is who I've been longing for!"

He was also well aware that this "woman" came from him. God chose not to create her from "the dust of the ground," like Adam. This beautiful creature was literally formed using a part of Adam's body. She was really made from "bone of his bone, and flesh of his flesh". This implies inseparable unity. This is the only way Eve could be directly related to Adam apart from childbirth. She was part of him. She was, in a sense, the rest of him. He was now complete.

How would your marriage be different if you viewed your wife the same way Adam viewed Eve – as "the rest of you?"

_____
_____
_____
_____

God has chosen to mysteriously meet certain needs in a man's life through an imperfect, challenging, ever-mystifying relationship with his wife.

It is amazing to think that – if YOU had been in the Garden of Eden, and God said it is not good for you to be alone – He would not have created anyone for you other than your wife.

Is that hard to fathom? _____ If you are honest, would you admit that you have ever wondered why He didn't give you someone else?

God is perfect, and does not make mistakes. He knows exactly what you need, and who is best suited to meet that need.

The grass is not, in fact, always greener on the other side of the fence. Fences have nothing to do with it. The grass is greenest where it is watered. ~Robert Fulghum

Crafted Prayer

Father, I must confess that there are times when I find it hard to fathom that _____ is Your perfect helper for me. Will You forgive me for doubting Your goodness, and Your perfect plan for my life?

Help me understand that she is uniquely designed to be Your instrument to help conform me into Your image, and make me the man You want me to be. Forgive me for ever being disappointed in or resentful of her.

With Your help Lord, I will lay down my self-seeking attitudes and selfish expectations, and try to trust You to be the Master of my life. I need Your help to lay aside my fears and let You take control. I know my wife is a major part of Your plan for me, and I need to embrace her as my completer, my "essential helper", not my adversary.

Lord, thank You for _____. She is Your daughter, and Your perfect provision for me.

The Almighty, Creator God, who loved Adam like no other created thing, knew that there was only one thing that would satisfy the deepest need in Adam's soul – woman.

Notes: *What did you hear God saying to you about your wife being the "rest of you" and His perfect provision for you?*

_____
_____
_____
_____
_____
_____
_____
_____
_____
_____
_____
_____

DAY 4

Matthew 19:6 - *So they are no longer two, but one. Therefore what God has joined together, let man not separate."*

Malachi 2:16 - *"I hate divorce," says the Lord God of Israel*

Marriage is not a contract; it is a covenant.

Marriage is God's idea. Divorce is not. Two people swear an oath to one another – to love, honor, cherish, in sickness and in health, till death do them part. They enter into a covenant relationship – before God.

A covenant is different than a contract. Our society would have us believe that marriage is a simple agreement that can be dissolved for "non performance". If one party doesn't live up to their end of the bargain – you just tear up the contract and walk your separate ways. It sounds so easy. But we all know it's not. The consequences of divorce have riddled our society like a machine gun.

As we discussed on Day 1, marriage is created by God and for God. Marriage is to be a representation to the world of God's covenant love for His bride – the church. It is little wonder why Satan is hell-bent on destroying Christian marriages. He is the sworn enemy of anything that glorifies God.

During the hard times in your marriage, you may have been tempted to think about life without her. Those thoughts come creeping in like cockroaches. It is critical that you know God's Word, how He values marriage and how He views divorce.

He doesn't say He hates people who get divorced, He says He hates divorce. As the designer of marriage and the One Who knows how blessed and fulfilled you will be if you allow Him to be the Lord of your marriage, it obviously breaks His heart when two people, who He brought together, decide to go their separate ways.

Have you ever been at a very difficult place in your marriage and given any thought to what divorce would look like? _____

At your wedding, you probably said things like "I promise to love, honor, and cherish you till death do us part." You swore an oath before God and those in attendance. Remember "in sickness and health, richer or poorer, etc" and "as long as we both shall live?" God takes oaths and covenants very seriously. Hebrews 13:4 says, "marriage should be honored (held in high esteem) by all".

Not only is marriage rarely recognized as God's precious gift, it is mocked and ridiculed in our modern culture as "old fashioned", and restrictive. With over 50% of today's marriages ending in divorce, the enemy is winning the battle and robbing couples, and their precious children, of the abundant life promised by Jesus.

There are over 280 references to "covenant" in the Bible. Here are only two:

Malachi 2:14
You ask, "Why?" It is because the Lord is acting as the witness between you and the wife of your youth, because you have broken faith with her, though she is your partner, the wife of your marriage covenant.

Proverbs 2:17
who has left the partner of her youth and ignored the covenant she made before God.

Can you think of other reasons why God would feel so deeply about divorce? _____
_____

Have you ever told your wife that you will never leave her, no matter what? Does she know that divorce will never be an option for you? _____

One of your wife's strongest emotional needs is security. She really needs to know that this is the way you feel about your covenant relationship with her. She will find great peace and safety knowing this is how you feel, and what you are committed to. It will also give her a stronger bond of trust in your heart and allow her to more freely give herself to you as well.

Action Step: In the next card you buy for your wife (anniversary, birthday, Valentine, etc.) tell her you want her to know you are committed to her, and to your marriage, for a lifetime.

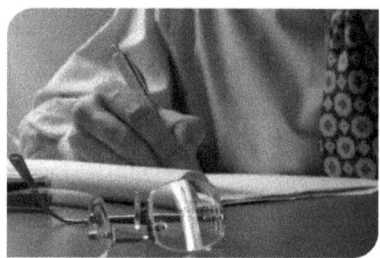

Crafted Prayer

Father, thank You that You are a covenant-keeping Father. You promise never to leave me or forsake me – no matter what. Your love for me and Your commitment to me aren't contingent on my performance. You chose me, adopted me into Your family, and there is nothing and no one who can ever change that. I am completely secure in our relationship.

Would You help me have that same level of security in my marriage relationship? Would You help me articulate my covenant love and commitment to my wife? I want her to know that I am committed to us, and to making our marriage everything You want it to be. I trust You God to give me the desire and the ability to see this through. You know things get difficult in our relationship, and my flesh wants out sometimes.

Please give me the courage and the will to love _____ like You love me, and help us enjoy the covenant relationship You have designed for us. I confess and renounce any thoughts I have ever had about leaving or divorce, or even daydreaming about someone or something else. I want what You have designed for me because I know that is what is best for me. I trust You Lord.

Deuteronomy 7:9
" Know therefore that the Lord your God is God; he is the faithful God, keeping his covenant of love to a thousand generations of those who love him and keep his commands."

Notes: *What did you hear God saying concerning your covenant relationship with your wife?*

_____
_____
_____
_____
_____
_____
_____
_____
_____
_____

DAY 5

Genesis 1:28 - *God blessed them and said to them, "Be fruitful and increase in number; fill the earth and subdue it. Rule over the fish of the sea and the birds of the air and over every living creature that moves on the ground."*

Alone, Adam was to tend a garden. As a couple, they were to "rule over" and "subdue the earth".

When Adam was alone in the garden God gave him meaningful work to do. He "worked and tended" the garden and also named all the animals (amazing). He was a busy man, yet he was a lonely and unfulfilled man. Neither the animals, nor his work could fill the void in his soul.

Amazingly, after God created Eve and brought her to Adam, He gave them work to do also. He gave them a mission, a purpose – together.

Have you ever considered the purpose God has for your marriage; what He may want to accomplish through the two of you that He couldn't accomplish with you individually? Any thoughts as to what that might be? The purpose is not just to have/raise kids. Think beyond that.

_____
_____
_____
_____

"Your marriage is foundational to your ministry."
~ Kevin Springer

There is something you have been given to do in this life that you can't accomplish alone. You have been given a great gift – a wife – with whom to partner in this great adventure with God. You are in this together!

What areas of life/ministry are you most passionate about at this point in your life? _____
_____
_____
_____

If money and time were no object, what would you most like to do with your life? _____
_____
_____
_____
_____

What areas of life/ministry is your wife most passionate about at this point in her life? _____
_____
_____
_____
_____

Crafted Prayer

Father, I must confess that I have been so busy, so preoccupied with my own life and agenda that I have given little thought to Your bigger picture. I have pursued my own adventure with little thought of the higher calling You are calling us to – together.

I know my marriage is by Your design, and that You have a higher, greater adventure for us as a couple. Would You please show me what that looks like? I really need You to reveal more to me, and to my wife, about what You are calling us to – together. Help us to make time to talk and dream together and seek You for what Your mission is for our marriage.

Help me to fully trust in Your plan for our life together. I have been too content with religious activities like going to church, or leading a class. Open my eyes to see the bigger picture for our marriage and, give me a heart that wants to follow You wherever You lead.

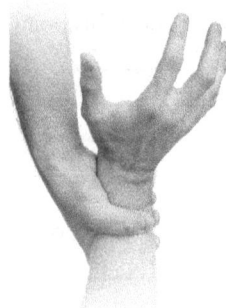

**Two are better than one,
because they have a good
return for their work:
If one falls down,
his friend can help him up.
But pity the man who falls
and has no one to help him up.
~Ecclesiastes 4:9-10**

Notes: *What did you hear God saying to you about your mission as a couple?*

_____
_____
_____
_____
_____
_____
_____
_____
_____

**"For I know the plans I have for you", declares the Lord,
"plans to prosper you and not to harm you, plans to give you
hope and a future." ~Jeremiah 29:11**

DAY 6

I Corinthians 7:28 - *But if you marry, you have not sinned; and if a virgin marries, she has not sinned. Yet such will have trouble in this life, and I am trying to spare you.*

The Bible tells us straight up that married people will have trouble in this life. Even though God created marriage for His glory and for our fulfillment, there was a fall. Because Adam and Eve chose to live life on their own terms and independent of God, life and marriage became hard. They have been hard ever since.

As a husband you are already personally familiar with this verse, even if you've never read it before. You have had, are having, and will have, troubles in this life as a married couple. They are part of life and part of marriage.

The key is to accept them as part of God's maturing process, and realize that the goal is not to avoid trouble, but to handle it in a Godly fashion. All couples struggle. The enemy will try to tell you that you two are the only ones who struggle with your issues. He will try to get you to keep quiet, stuff your feelings deep in the basement of your soul, and hope they go away. Trouble is… they don't.

List two troubles you are experiencing currently in your marriage, and what you are doing about them:

1. _____
   _____

2. _____
   _____

Even though a Google search will reveal some of the "Top 10 Reasons People Get Married" as: legitimate sex, cultural acceptance, financial stability, etc., most couples would say the reasons they got married were for a) love, and b) happiness. They feel great love and affection for another person - and that person makes them feel really happy. We all naturally (and naively) assume these feelings will last a lifetime.

For most couples these feelings do last a while, but some begin to face the reality of fading emotions as early as their honeymoon. God specifically tells us that we will experience trouble in our married life together. If we are relying on feelings, those troubles will arrive early, and can seem insurmountable.

Your expectations get trampled. You begin to see a side of your wife you didn't know she had. You both begin to unpack your life's baggage, and it doesn't look very pretty.

What do you do then? Men will typically do one of three things - You angrily vocalize your disappointments, which results in arguments and hurt feelings, or you stuff them deep in your heart and hope things get better with time, or with God's help you learn to communicate about them and get them resolved. If not resolved, those disappointments eventually turn into resentments, and one day they erupt in a firestorm of destruction.

God is not telling you to avoid marriage, or to ignore your feelings. He is simply telling you that trouble is a part of life together. Financial troubles, children troubles, sickness, heartache, feelings of love that rise and fall, emotional turmoil, in-laws, you name it –

trouble is just part of it. He is reminding you that He is the anchor, the fortress, the high tower you run to when those troubles come. You need to send down deep spiritual roots early in your marriage that can sustain you when the winds of trouble come – because they do come.

He also wants you to talk about your issues and work through them together. An integral part of experiencing oneness in marriage is learning how to communicate effectively and to lovingly resolve conflict. There are many excellent books, seminars and classes that cover these topics in greater detail, and I would highly recommend you check out our "Additional Resources" page for help.

Crafted Prayer

Father, thank You that it is You that I can count on when trouble comes my way. You are always there; always listening, and You always have the answer if I will just listen – and follow. Forgive me for relying on my emotions instead of upon Your Word and Your provision for me and my marriage. Help me lock arms with my wife when trouble comes and run to You for refuge. Thank You that You allow trouble into our marriage in order to shape me into the man You intend me to be, and to keep me from relying on myself, or other things, for solutions. You're a great God.

Lord, You know the troubles I am experiencing in my marriage right now. I give each of them to You (bring up each one by name) and trust You to help me through them. I need Your wisdom, patience, strength and direction in order to have victory over these. Speak to me Lord, and give me the courage to obey what You tell me to do.

I love my wife Lord, and I desire to be the husband she needs, and that You require. Help me not blame her for my troubles, and to view her as Your divine provision and partner. Thank You that You are here with me right now, and that You care about every detail of my life. I lay my troubles and cares at Your feet and know You have everything I need to triumph over them.

Notes: *What is God speaking to you about handling the troubles in your marriage?*

_____
_____
_____
_____
_____
_____
_____
_____
_____
_____
_____
_____
_____

"A good marriage is the union of two forgivers."
~ Ruth Bell Graham

DAY 7

I Corinthians 7:33-34 - *but one who is married is concerned about the things of the world, how he may please his wife, and his interests are divided. The woman who is unmarried, and the virgin, is concerned about the things of the Lord, that she may be holy both in body and spirit; but one who is married is concerned about the things of the world, how she may please her husband.*

Notice that the primary concern in this life, for a married man, is his wife. The primary concern of the married woman is her husband. Yes, that is how things *should* be. Would you say that the primary concern of your life right now – is your spouse?

If not, there are some adjustments that need to be made. What really are your primary concerns in this life? Bills, saving for retirement, health, losing weight, disciplining your kids, ministry or job pressures? There are dozens of them aren't there? This verse is telling husbands that the proper priority for your marriage relationship, and the needs of your wife – is #1 on the list. The other things are real and important concerns, but ahead of them all – should be *pleasing your wife*.

Note: We assume here that as a Christian man, you already understand that your daily walk with Christ is your top priority – period. We will talk about this more in the days ahead. Your top *earthly* priority though – is to please your wife.

In order to please your wife – you must somehow figure out what it takes to please her. What are her needs? What makes her happy? Most men don't really know the answer to these questions. They will assume things based on television, movies, magazines, or what others have said – but, what about your unique spouse? Have you ever asked her?

Action Step: Find a few minutes to get alone with your wife. Read today's verse out loud, then ask her - what are three ways I can please you more in our relationship? Write down her responses so you have a reminder.

1. _____

2. _____

3. _____

The fear in asking is that you may hear something you don't want to hear. *It would please me greatly if you would spend more time with me and the kids. It would really make me happy if you would help me more around the house.* You need to ask, and you need to be ready to respond in love (and in obedience to God) to whatever your wife says is a legitimate way to please her.

Here is a list from "Husband- A User's Guide," to refresh your memory:

Basic Needs of a Wife

1. A wife needs a husband who is committed to her and their marriage – no matter what.

2. A wife needs a husband who is walking with Jesus and trying to lead her spiritually.

3. A wife needs a husband who praises her and makes her feel special.

4. A wife needs a husband who values and cherishes her.

5. A wife needs a husband who provides for her and makes her feel secure, emotionally as well as financially.

6. A wife needs a husband who protects her – physically, emotionally and spiritually.

7. A wife needs a husband who listens and allows her to process life.

8. A wife needs a husband who communicates with her and allows her into his world.

9. A wife needs a husband who invests in her life and invites her to flourish as a person.

10. A wife needs to know that she is meeting her husband's vital needs.

How are you doing? How many of these ten needs would you say you are doing well? _____

Another courageous move on your part would be to talk through this list with your wife, and then (gulp) ask her how you are doing, or which one(s) you can specifically work on.

A husband's and wife's primary needs typically fall into the following categories:

Affection, Sexual Fulfillment, Meaningful Conversation, Recreational Companionship, Honesty and Openness, Physical Attractiveness, Financial Support, Domestic Support, Marriage/Family Commitment and Admiration/Respect

> *Dear children, let us not love with words or tongue, but with actions and in truth.*
> *~1 John 3:18*

This would also be a great list for both of you to review together and openly discuss what your needs really are.

Crafted Prayer

Lord, this marriage thing is very hard. You call me to live a very unselfish life, and to give up a lot for my wife. I want to be obedient, but I am telling you now that I really don't always feel like loving and pleasing my wife, or putting her needs above my own. I really need You to create in me a deeper desire to do the things You call me to do. I want to want to.

I need Your help to give me the courage to ask hard questions, and to change my selfish ways if I ever hope to be the husband You are calling me to be. Help me be better at communicating and show me how to be a more attentive, sincere listener. Help me give her the time she wants, and grant me the courage to open up more of my life (thoughts, dreams, fears, etc.) to her. I really need You to help me make her my #1 earthly priority. Show me how to do this today, Lord. Thank You.

Notes: *What is God speaking to you about pleasing your wife?*

_____
_____
_____
_____
_____
_____

> **"The Christian is supposed to love his neighbor,
> and since his wife is his nearest neighbor,
> she should be his deepest love."
> ~ Martin Luther**

DAY 8

Romans 12:10 - *Be devoted to one another in brotherly love. Honor one another above yourselves.*

A major way to please your wife is to show her how important she is to you. *Dedicated. Loyal. Committed* - are other terms you may recognize as synonyms for "devoted". God calls each of us to be devoted to our wife. How is it that some of us find it easier to be devoted to our golfing/hunting buddies than to our wife? Some of us will work for hours on a duck blind, or fishing trip, but can't seem to find the energy to get up off the recliner to help our wife put away some groceries.

Are you devoted to your wife? What personal priorities do you place above hers? What people or events are ahead of her on your list of "must-dos" today?

Like love, the word "devoted" speaks of action. What does devotion look like? You made vows of devotion at the marriage altar, but is that all she gets? I promise to love, honor, etc. etc.? The verse above goes on to speak of honoring your spouse above yourself. This is beginning to sound like work might be involved. What was God thinking?

Yes, we all voiced our devotion to our wife when we said "I do". Since then we have covered ourselves in work, kids, bills, hobbies, etc., and those ceremonial words have grown a little cold. For many, they have completely frozen. God is calling you to actually show your devotion; to honor Him by doing what He calls you to do.

List three things that would show your devotion to your wife, and honor her as the #1 love of your life?

1. _____

2. _____

3. _____

Action Step: Sometime this week, without being asked, and without expecting anything in return (a thank you, or sex) - do the dishes (or at least help put your dishes away), vacuum the floor; take out the trash; pick up your clothes; make the bed; take out the dog; keep the kids and let her have a day/night out with friends; do something romantic like send her a card, email or text to tell her you love her and were just thinking about her, or buy her flowers, or rub her tired feet or back while watching TV.

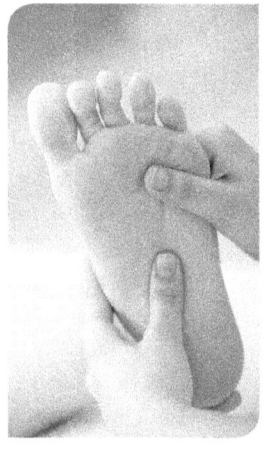

What do you think it looks like to "honor your wife"?

_____
_____
_____
_____

How often do you praise your wife? Can you think of the last time you praised her in front of the kids, or your friends, or her parents?

We all need praise. We need to know that our life matters and that people notice the good things we try to do. Who better to praise kids than their parents? Who better to praise your wife than her husband? Don't wait for some other guy to do it, or she will be attracted to that, and maybe even to him.

List three things you can praise your wife for – today.

1. _____
2. _____
3. _____

Cultivate the habit of praise. Praise your wife openly and often. Let the world know what a fabulous gift from God she is, and what she is doing well. Yes, she is still a work in progress (as are you), but you are told by God to honor (praise, appreciate, esteem) her anyway.

Remember – He is the One Who made her and brought her specifically to you. When you choose not to honor her, you are really choosing not to honor/thank Him.

Crafted Prayer

Father, help me to want to be more devoted to my wife. Show me what I can do to put her needs above my own. Speak to me about how I can show my devotion in practical, meaningful ways. Forgive me for my self-centeredness, and for secretly insisting on her changing before I am willing to obey You in this.

Help me Lord to love her as you have loved me; unselfishly and unconditionally – and help me start today. Give me the courage to obey You and make choices to put her needs ahead of mine. Give me the grace to say "no" to some things I have considered more fun or personally fulfilling, and to choose my wife's happiness over my own.

Lead me in my attempts to hear from You and follow what You tell me to do. Grant me the courage to do what You say, and to trust that "he who loves his wife, loves himself". I know You will reward me as I obey You and put this into practice.

Notes: *What is God speaking to you being devoted to, and honoring your wife?*

_____
_____
_____
_____
_____
_____
_____
_____

**The man who finds a wife finds a treasure,
and he receives favor from the Lord.
~ Proverbs 18:22**

DAY 9

John 13:34 - *"A new command I give you: Love one another. As I have loved you, so you must love one another".*

Ephesians 5:25 - *Husbands, love your wives, just as Christ loved the church and gave himself up for her…*

Colossians 3:19 - *Husbands, love your wives and do not be harsh with them.*

Did you notice the word Jesus uses in the first sentence? "Command". Yes, He commands us to love one another. As followers of His, He expects us to follow His commands. This is not just a holy suggestion for our consideration. As a spouse, we are commanded to love each other. This carries as much weight as "Thou shalt not…".

He goes on to use the same command when speaking to husbands concerning loving their wives. You are commanded to love your wife, "just like" Christ loved the church (His bride). For years I didn't really "get" this. I was aware of the words, but they didn't carry the appropriate weight to me. They also carry the same consequences.

If you deliberately disobey God's laws/commandments there are consequences. It is true with stealing, murder, adultery – and it is true with not loving your wife. With God, it is not an option to use the excuse, "But, you don't know my wife". He actually does know her.

You see, He created her specifically for you. She is God's special gift to you and it breaks His heart for you to reject such a thoughtful gift. Yes, your wife can be a royal challenge sometimes, but that is no excuse for not doing what you have been commanded to do. Reading these passages will also reveal that there is no "if she", or "when she", or "because she" caveat (excuse) present in any verse.

So, does God call you, even command you, to love your spouse knowing full well that she will quite often act unlovable? **Yes.**

Actually, He uses Himself as the example. He left all the comforts and glory of heaven to come to earth as a helpless mortal. He learned to obey his parents. He experienced peer pressure and teasing as a kid. He went through puberty. He went to school, studied, and got tested on subjects that He had created himself. He mentored 12 men who often drove him batty. They were stubborn, selfish and plain dense at times. He endured verbal and physical abuse that he didn't deserve. He finally died a cruel and excruciating death. And why?

He is the definition and the personification of love. He showed us how to love the unlovable and undeserving. He did it. He didn't just talk about it. So how lame does it sound to Him to say…. She isn't treating me very nicely or being very respectful or loving. So, how did Jesus do it?

He had help. Only with the Father's help could Jesus live the life he lived and die the death he died. It is the same for you. It is only as you abide in Him that you can experience the power to love others as He loved us.

How do you typically respond when your wife isn't acting very loving or respectful towards you? _____
_____
_____

Have you ever found yourself wanting to throw up your hands and say, "I just can't do this?" _____

If so – great! That is exactly where God wants you. He never meant for you to try your best to make marriage work, or to be a successful husband on your own. God's design for marriage was for a husband and wife to partner with Him in every aspect of their life together. Marriage was never designed to be lived apart from His daily involvement, wisdom, direction and power.

> **"You can't possibly master enough principals
> and disciplines to ensure that your life works out.
> You weren't meant to and God won't let you."**
> ~ John Eldredge, Walking with God

Crafted Prayer

Jesus, I am amazed by your love for me. I am so unworthy of your love, and yet you tell me that I am precious to you. Thank you for dying a painful death so that I can enjoy an abundant life – with You, both now and for eternity. Would You fill me with the power I need to love my wife as You have loved me? Help me see her through your eyes of love. Help me love her in spite of how she reacts, responds or treats me.

Lord, I need You to remind me that it is a command that I love my wife, regardless to her performance or response. I choose to love her even when I don't feel loving. I choose to forgive her even if she doesn't ask for it. She is my essential helper and a gift from Your hand. Thank You for her. Give me eyes to see her as You see her, and to love her as I should. Forgive me again for not appreciating Your wonderful provision in her. With Your help, I will love her better today.

Notes: *What did you hear God saying concerning His command to love your wife as Christ loved the church?*

DAY 10

Luke 18:27 - *"What is impossible with men is possible with God."*

Jeremiah 32:27 - *"Behold, I am the Lord, the God of all flesh; is anything too difficult for Me?"*

There are times in every marriage when you don't feel much like loving your wife, and other times when life's problems just get you down. No matter what your marriage trouble – God is bigger. There is nothing too big for Him.

Some of you feel that you are in an impossible situation right now. Adultery, addiction, depression, and others are formidable foes. God states very clearly in these verses that nothing is too difficult for Him to handle, and nothing is impossible for Him to restore or fix. Do we really believe that though? You want to, but many of you really don't. You may have decided that what you are experiencing is just too big for anyone, even God.

Write down the most desperate need in your marriage.
_____
_____

Now, write down how you would like God to handle this situation.
_____
_____
_____
_____

Realizing that many times God doesn't answer your prayer in the exact way you ask, are you willing to accept God's way (over your way) of answering it – even if His answer is "wait", or "no"? God is not out to get you or punish you. He loves you. He likes you. He wants only what is best for you – really.

The primary temptation Satan used on Eve in the Garden of Eden was to get her to doubt God's goodness. "Did God really say…?" All of his schemes were designed to get Eve (and Adam) to doubt God's love and to question whether He had their best interests at heart. Satan convinced them that God could not be trusted and that they had better take matters into their own hands. They did, and with devastating consequences.

If you really understand the love of God for you, you would be completely free to trust Him with every issue and circumstance in your life. The Bible says He has "good plans for you", yet many of you actually fear He will "mess up" your life if you really turn it over to His control.

Do you really believe God loves and accepts you unconditionally? _____

Do you truly believe that His plans for you are always for your good? _____

Do you believe He is big enough to handle the need you wrote down above? _____

If you answered any of these questions "No", you are honest. God loves honesty. It's okay to doubt. It's okay to question. God can handle it.

Pray the Crafted Prayer that follows, and tell God whether you believe it or not. God loves to astonish His people with magnificent displays of grace and love. He is an extravagant Father.

Don't let doubt or apprehension keep you stuck. Keep on going through the Challenge, and ask God to increase your faith and trust in Him. That kind of prayer He always answers – "Yes".

Crafted Prayer

Father, Your Word says there is nothing too big for You to handle. Whether or not I believe that doesn't make it any less true. You know I have troubles I need Your help with. I have tried and tried and can't seem to gain any victory. I really need You, Lord.

I want to believe that "nothing is impossible for You". Would You help my unbelief? Would You give me more faith, more trust, and more hope in Your goodness and faithfulness towards me? Would you allow me to see Your hand at work in my life – in a tangible way? I am desperate for You.

Thank you that You love me. Thank You that there is nothing I can do to make You love me any more than You already do. I don't have to perform for You. I don't have to tap dance for Your approval. You love me – period. I am so undeserving, and I am overwhelmed by Your affection for me.

I am so thankful to serve a God that is always bigger than any need I have. I am thrilled to be your son. Thank you for choosing me, for adopting me into Your family, and for restoring the chance to have a daily, moment-by-moment relationship with You.

Psalm 34:4
I sought the Lord, and He answered me,
And delivered me from all my fears.

Notes: *What did you hear God saying concerning His majesty, strength and ability to meet any need in your life and marriage?*

_____
_____
_____
_____
_____
_____

_____
_____
_____
_____
_____
_____
_____
_____
_____

**We have to pray with our eyes on God,
not on the difficulties. ~ Oswald Chambers**

DAY 11

John 15:5 - *"I am the vine; you are the branches. The one who remains in Me and I in him produces much fruit, because you can do nothing without Me."*

The Secret Jesus Knew – is the first thing you have to realize about life, and about your marriage - *You can't do this alone.* You were not created to live life apart from a daily, moment-by-moment walk with God Himself. Remember, you can't learn enough rules for successful living, or principles for a happy marriage to make life work out. You weren't meant to. If you could, then you would get the credit for your success and not God.

What you were meant to do is live in constant fellowship with your Creator. It was so in Eden and, because of Jesus, it is possible now. As a Christian, your sin no longer separates you from God's loving presence. He is the branch – the source of all you need for life. He has all the wisdom, patience, understanding and power to help you be the husband you truly want to be. You will only produce fruit in your life, and in your marriage, as you abide in (dwell, stay attached to) Him. No abiding – no fruit.

Back on Day 9 we asked the question, how did Jesus do it? How was He able to love and forgive the people who tortured and killed Him?

Like our verse for today, several times in the Book of John, Jesus says that he could "do nothing" also. He didn't have any supernatural powers when He was here in earth. He only did what he saw the Father doing, and he only said what he heard the Father say. No wonder he "arose a great while before day" to pray (Mark 1:35), and often slipped away from his disciples to pray for hours. He was desperate to know what he was supposed to do next. We should be the same way. If Jesus couldn't live and minister successfully without staying attached to "the vine", who are we to think we can?

Is it hard to realize that you cannot do life, or marriage, well without help? _____

What areas of your life and marriage have you felt the need to control? _____
_____
_____

Men are notorious for compartmentalizing our lives. We can trust God with our "Christian" compartment – church, leading a small group, etc., but what about our job, our money, our vacation plans, our daily "to do" list, our sex life, our hobbies? Now, that's hitting below the belt.

Not really, according to God. Christ died to become your Savior and provide the opportunity for you to live with God in eternity, but He also desires to be your Lord. You can't "serve two masters", so you have to decide to be your own master, or to allow Him to be. There is no neutral ground. You are either running your own life, or you are allowing Him to. You either live your life with your face toward God, or your back toward God.

Is Christ really Lord of your life – all of your life? _____ Have you felt like you should be able to give God your Christian compartments (church, small group, etc.) and then you should be able to run the rest of your life?

What area(s) of your life is He bringing to your mind right now that you need to surrender to His leadership? _____
_____

A branch, separated from the vine will slowly wither and die. Such is the life, and marriage, of those who choose to detach themselves from the Source of life. They look okay for a while, but over time their fruit falls off, their life becomes barren, and they lose the very life they so longed for.

Unlike a branch made of wood, you can reattach to the Vine. When you finally reach the end of your rope and throw in the towel – God is standing right there (He never moved). He will willingly and lovingly allow you to reattach to His life source and He will begin to send abundant life flowing through you again.

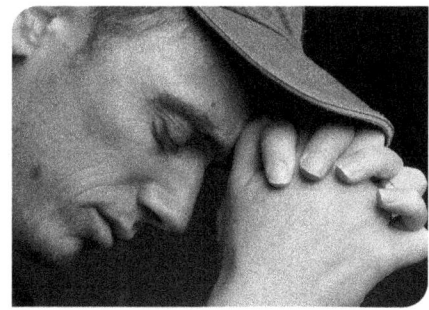

All it takes is a change of mind, and a sincere desire to turn away from your desire to run your own life, your way. The Bible calls this "repentance". Simply turn to Him, tell Him you're sorry for thinking you know better how to run your life than He does, and ask Him to forgive and restore you.

Crafted Prayer

Father, I ask You right now to please forgive me. Forgive me for thinking I can run my life better than You. I have made a mess of things and I really need Your help. Would You lead me from this point forward? Would You take control of my life, my plans, my agenda and my marriage? I trust You to do what is best and to lead me to a better place.

Please restore my hope and return my joy. I ask You to be the Lord and Master of my life. I confess that I have tried to control certain areas of my life and have not asked, or trusted You to be Lord of them.

Thank you, that You are a God of fresh starts. Thank You for forgiving me, and for being willing to be involved in every aspect of my life and marriage. I willingly turn over all of my life to You. Help me to trust You and Your sovereign plans for my life today and every day.

Matthew 7:11

"If you then, being evil, know how to give good gifts to your children, how much more will your Father who is in heaven give what is good to those who ask Him!"

Notes: *What did you hear God saying concerning Him being your source of life, and Lord of it?*

DAY 12

Joshua 24:15 - But if you refuse to serve the Lord, then choose today whom you will serve. Would you prefer the gods your ancestors served beyond the Euphrates? Or will it be the gods of the Amorites in whose land you now live? But as for me and my family, we will serve the Lord."

Even though you now know that you can do nothing without Christ, there is something you can do, and you do it every day – choose. You make hundreds of choices every day. You will decide whether or not to get out of bed early to spend time with your heavenly Father. You will decide to have a cheerful, loving attitude toward your wife and children. You will decide to spend time in God's Word. Everything from what to eat for breakfast to how fast to drive to work; from what clothes to wear today to what television shows to watch tonight – your life is a series of choices.

The primary choice facing each of us every sunrise, and throughout every day of our lives, is whether or not to let Christ be Lord of our life, or run things our way. Who will it be? You get to decide. Your life is a series of days, and your days are a series of choices. The choices you make today will affect your entire life.

The Bible says "you cannot serve two masters". There is no middle ground. You are either the ruler of your domain, or you allow Christ to rule. This is not a one-time prayer, or confession. This happens every day, and throughout the day – for a lifetime.

After years of counseling and mentoring married couples, it is abundantly clear that one thing is absolutely necessary in order for you and me to have a successful life, and a successful, fulfilling marriage – choosing to become deliberate.

You must become a deliberate Christ-follower (Christian) if you are to ever experience the abundant life promised by Jesus. It will not happen on its own, or without effort. Your marriage will never be what you desire it to be unless you choose to be a deliberate husband. Both of these choices must dominate your mindset. Everything else in your life must take second place to them, and depend on them.

Would you say you are walking today as a deliberate Christian? Are you practicing being a deliberate husband? List two examples of each:

1. _____
2. _____
1. _____
2. _____

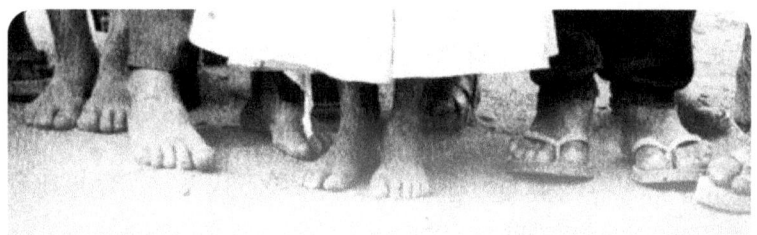

Jesus told His disciples, "If anyone would come after me, he must deny himself and take up his cross daily and follow me." It is crystal clear, that to follow Christ you must continually make three choices – deny yourself (your right to run your life), take up your cross daily (die to your rights) and follow me (follow His lead, not lead out on your own).

Jesus never asked anyone to clean up their act and then follow Him. He never told anyone to learn more or serve more. All He asks is for us to make a conscious choice, every day, to lay down our independence and trust Him as Lord of our life.

Also noteworthy is the fact that following Christ is not about being religious. It is not about going to church, or teaching Sunday School, or even giving your money. All are wonderful Biblical practices, but do not necessarily constitute walking with Jesus. Listen to what Jesus said to the most religious, Biblically-scholared, synagogue-attending people of His day:

You diligently study the Scriptures because you think that by them you possess eternal life. These are the Scriptures that testify about me, yet you refuse to come to me to have life. **John 5:39-40**

Read also what Jesus says about many religious people at the end times:

Many will say to Me on that day, Lord, Lord, have we not prophesied in Your name and driven out demons in Your name and done many mighty works in Your name? And then I will say to them openly (publicly), I never knew you; depart from Me. **John 7:22-23**

Becoming a deliberate Christian involves choosing a relationship over religion. In both of the Scriptures above, Christ said that life, both here and eternal, is about Him – knowing Him, as a person. As in any relationship, it takes time together to blossom. Choose today to get to know Jesus, the person, the shepherd, the way, the truth, the life, the Prince of Peace. You will be amazed by Him.

Crafted Prayer

Lord, I confess that I have not been very deliberate in following You, or in being a husband. Please forgive me for my apathy, and help me in this area. Do a deep work in me to develop more of a passion for knowing You, and spending time with You. I know it breaks Your heart that I have been so fickle.

As Your Word says in Philippians 2:13, it is You that works in me both to will and to do of Your good pleasure. Please do a new work in me and give me the desire to do Your will. I want to follow You and experience the adventure of watching You lead my life and my marriage. Help me get out of the way and yield my rights to You, so You can do what is best for me and for my family.

Today I choose You. I choose to give You my heart, my life, my marriage and my future. I choose to follow You. Remind me by Your Holy Spirit to continue to choose You throughout this day, and all those that follow. I want my life to count. I want my marriage to count. Help me Lord. Thank You.

Notes: *What did you hear God saying to you about becoming a deliberate follower and husband?*

_____
_____
_____
_____
_____
_____
_____

Your marriage will be as fulfilling as your walk with Jesus
~ Rob Thorpe

DAY 13

I Peter 3:7 - *Husbands, in the same way be considerate as you live with your wives, and treat them with respect as the weaker partner and as heirs with you of the gracious gift of life, so that nothing will hinder your prayers.*

As a deliberate follower of Christ, and as a deliberate husband, you have to choose every day to obey God's Word in your life. In this verse, Peter is speaking of being considerate as you live with your wife. Other translations use the word "understanding." It calls for understanding, sensitivity, and meeting your wife's needs. It involves a sincere effort to understand her desires, feelings, fears, concerns, anxieties, goals, and dreams.

Mainly, it boils down to knowing her. You need to become a student of your wife. You need to read about marriage, attend marriage classes and seminars to try to better understand her. You need to deliberately and actively listen to her and ask God daily to help you better understand her heart. Remember, the best way to get to know someone is to simply spend time with them.

What do you think your wife's two greatest concerns in life are today? _____
_____
_____

> **The great question... which I have not been able to answer... is, "What does a woman want?" ~ Freud**

True understanding takes time. Learning a new language, learning to play a musical instrument or even trying to understand my new iPad – all take time. God will also give you understanding if you ask Him - **2 Tim. 2:7** - *Consider what I say, for the Lord will give you understanding in everything.*

I have been married over thirty five years and am still learning and growing in my understanding of how my wife works. I do feel that I understand her much better than I did early in our marriage – because we have spent so much time together. Sadly, I have also learned a lot from doing things the wrong way. I read several books on marriage/relationships every year, and will never completely understand the heart/mind of a woman. But I am trying, and growing, and my wife notices and really appreciates it. It makes her feel valued.

What are two things you wish you better understood about your wife? _____
_____
_____

One of the best ways to begin to understand your wife's heart is to spend some time talking with her about her life.

Action Step: Schedule a date, or some one-on-one time just to get together and talk about your life together. Here are some questions you can throw out for discussion:

1. What do you think we could do to have a better marriage?
2. What can I do to be a better father to our kids?
3. Where do you see our lives in 5, 10 years?
4. What areas of life or ministry do you feel like you're missing out on? Why?
5. What makes you really happy / sad right now?
6. How can I help you be more fulfilled as a woman?
7. What mission/ministry do you feel God has in store for us together?

When you have opportunities to talk with your wife, ask questions that evoke emotion. These type questions use phrases like, "how do you feel about…", and "why do you think…". Remember, your wife talks about a problem primarily to process her emotions, not her thoughts. She's not wasting words or time. Most of the time she is not even wanting to reach a conclusion or have you "fix" the problem. This is where you can develop the fine art of active listening. No newspaper, no television, no iPhone, just you and her, looking into her eyes and listening.

Try to listen for her emotions, (her heart) as she talks. What is she feeling, and why? She thinks and processes differently than you. Keep in mind that it was God Who created these communication differences and you need to seek Him for wisdom to better understand them. This too is a deliberate, continual process and an integral part of achieving oneness.

Read today's verse again, and pay particular attention to the consequence of treating your wife this way, or choosing not to. The verse concludes with the statement, "so nothing will hinder your prayers". The word hinder means to, *frustrate, impede* or *retard*. The idea is that failure to treat your wife with understanding will get in the way of and hamper your attempts to pray. Your prayers to God will be "done away with," "frustrated," and "impeded."

Mark it down: A husband's domestic relationship with his wife has a profound impact on his spiritual fellowship with God! A husband's spiritual fellowship with God has a profound impact on his domestic relationship with his wife!

Crafted Prayer

Father, I confess that so many times when my wife wants to talk, I am so not wanting to listen. I am so not interested, or so distracted and want to get back to "my" life and thoughts.

Forgive me Lord for not being more attentive, more understanding, and more loving with her. She is a gift from You and I have not treated her as such. Forgive me for being so selfish.

Today, would you help me be more attentive to my wife's heart? Help me to make time to talk with her and give me the patience and grace to truly listen and to care about her world and her feelings. Show me any area in my life where I am failing You and failing her. I want to be the best husband on the planet.

Notes: *What did you hear God saying to you about living with your wife in an understanding way?*

_____
_____
_____
_____
_____
_____
_____

DAY 14

I Corinthians 9:24 - Do you not know that those who run in a race all run, but only one receives the prize? Run in such a way that you may win.

Are you running the marriage "race" to win? Are you working hard to be the best marriage partner you can be?

Most of us find ourselves running, because we're married. So, we're in the "race". Question is – are we going to limp along and be content with being a participant – or are we willing to put in the hard work to be the winner? When my oldest son was in elementary school, the private Christian school was often needing to raise money. Twice a year they would hold a "jog-a-thon". The little kids would seek out donors to pay a small amount of money for every lap they ran around the jog-a-thon track.

Every kid who ran in the jog-a-thon received a "participant" ribbon, whether they ran one lap or a hundred. No one's fragile personality was harmed as they all got a ribbon. One kid, however, received special recognition (and a shiny trophy) for finishing first (running the most laps). You guessed it, my son could have cared less about being a participant – he wanted to win the thing. It didn't matter if it was bitter cold or sweltering hot, he would run around that huge parking lot until he was declared the winner. We still have those little trophies in our attic today.

As a husband, are you just a participant, or do you intend to do whatever it takes to win at marriage?

Can you think of other endeavors or hobbies where you try to excel? Name a couple:

1. _____ 2. _____

Sadly, most married couples today find themselves in the bleachers, admiring as a few world-class marriages move ahead in life, while they eat the nachos and soft drinks of life. Marriage, like most everything worth having or doing well in life, requires hard work. More than half don't make it the first time around. Only one in four make it the second time.

It is not enough to say vows that affirm that "Christ is the center of our home", and "before God and these witnesses" at our wedding ceremony. It's not enough to go to church regularly, or even teach Sunday school, or work with the youth. A great marriage relationship is not dependent on any of these. God calls you to a life surrendered to His will and His agenda for you. He asks you to follow Him, not charge through your life your way, and ask Him to bless it or bail you out when you get in trouble.

How many books about marriage and relationships have you read over the last year? _____ Have you attended any marriage classes or seminars? What about reading blogs or listening to podcasts about marriage? More importantly, how much time during the week do you spend praying for your wife and for your marriage? _____

Are you working hard at making her your #1 priority, and living with her *"in an understanding way"*? We all need to become students of our wife. We need to walk deliberately each and every day with the God Who made us, and is willing to walk and talk with us, and give us everything we need. We need to read His Word. We need to read all we can about the opposite sex, and marriage, and relationships. We need to try and understand better how to be the best at this "race" we have been called to. It takes work, discipline, and time – lots of time. Don't settle for "okay". Run in such a way as to say – "I was the best husband I could be." Are you content with a participant ribbon?

On a scale of 1-10 (ten being the highest), how would you rate the current effort/diligence you put in on your marriage?

_____

What are the primary priorities keeping you from running the marriage race to win it? _____
_____
_____
_____
_____
_____
_____

The avid hunters I know, spend lots of time shooting, cleaning their guns, building their blinds, training their retrievers, etc. The avid golfers I know spend hours on the practice range, and spend plenty of money on balls, clubs, accessories, lessons, etc.

How are you investing in better understanding your wife, and having a world-class marriage?_____

One day, we will all be held accountable by God for how well we did at being a husband. He will not ask us about our golf game, or the 12 point buck that used to hang on the wall.

Crafted Prayer

Father, I am convicted by how little effort I put into having the kind of marriage that would truly glorify You, and fulfill my wife. Forgive me for my laziness. Forgive me for putting a greater priority on other earthly pursuits ahead of those that really matter.

Would You teach me? Would You walk with me, and counsel me, and give me the wisdom and stamina to run this race to win? I desperately need You power to energize me and help me do what it takes. I need Your encouragement today Lord. Help me be the best husband on the planet.

Today, help me to begin running the race to win. I don't want to be content with an "okay" marriage. I want to have a great marriage but I know it will take sacrifice and hard work on my part. Give me the energy and determination to follow through, even when I don't feel like it or see results. I trust You Lord, and know You are cheering for me. Help me be a winning husband.

Notes: *What did you hear God saying to you about running the marriage race to win?*

_____
_____
_____
_____
_____
_____
_____
_____

DAY 15

Colossians 3:13 - Bear with each other and forgive whatever grievances you may have against one another. Forgive as the Lord forgave you.

An unforgiving heart clings to the past, refusing to extend to others what your heavenly Father has extended to you. A resentful, unforgiving attitude results in all manner of negative consequences. Research has shown that this attitude results in both physical and mental problems, including chronic pain, cardiovascular problems, violent behavior, hopelessness, anxiety, depression and suicide.

One of the most significant repercussions of unforgiveness is that bitterness takes root in your heart, and then spreads its poison to choke out every godly trait there. The truth is – if you choose to be unforgiving—it is a deliberate decision and a self-inflicted wound. You carry the illusion that other people have caused your misery, but in reality, you have elected to take on a form of self-imposed bondage. You are the one suffering for your unforgiveness, not the other person.

God knows that unforgiveness, bitterness and resentment can bind you like heavy chains and choke off the abundant life He promises you. He loves you and doesn't want you to live like that. This is why He urges you to get rid of these.

More importantly, Jesus said in **Mark 11:26** – "But if you do not forgive, neither will your Father who is in heaven forgive your transgressions." If you don't choose to forgive, Jesus says the Father won't forgive you. That ought to make chills run down your spine. It is critical that you learn to forgive your wife when she lets you down, or says/does something to hurt you, or doesn't meet your expectations. You will suffer the consequences if you don't – not her.

You are to forgive your wife – "as the Lord forgave you." That is the standard before you. How did Jesus forgive the people who beat him, spit on him and stripped the flesh off of his back? Completely. Unconditionally.

You already know this – but you can't do that without God's help. Only He can give you the grace and love to forgive like He does.

List two things that you need to forgive your wife for:

1. _____ 2. _____

Are there other people who come to mind (father, mother, sibling, friend, etc.) that you need to forgive, and let go of the hurt, anger and pain they have caused in your past? _____

> "When you hold resentment toward another, you are bound to that person or condition by an emotional link that is stronger than steel. Forgiveness is the only way to dissolve that link and get free." ~ Catherine Ponder

Forgiveness is a choice, not a feeling. You may not feel like forgiving your wife, or someone else who has hurt you in your past, but you can choose to do so. I'm sure Jesus wasn't feeling like forgiving the soldiers who just nailed giant spikes through his hands and feet – but he did.

Action Step: Get alone with God today and take a sheet of paper and a pen with you. Write down every hurtful thing anyone has ever done or said to you on that paper. Take your time. Listen to God. Ask Him to bring things back to your mind that you have tried to forget. No, it doesn't feel good, but this will set you free if you stick with it.

After listing everything you can think of, go down the list <u>one at a time</u> and, as an act of your will, **say this out loud**:

> "Thank You Father, that by Your grace I can now choose to forgive _____ for _____ _____. I release them to You, and I ask that You forgive them also. I renounce any bitterness, unforgiveness, anger and resentment that I have felt toward _____, and announce that I am free from those emotions and from the chains that have bound me. I am free in Christ. I am no longer under the power of these acts and memories. Thank You Jesus, for shedding Your blood for me and for all the hurt I have ever suffered. I am free in You!"

When you are through, either tear your paper up into tiny pieces, or find a place to safely burn it. When you do, you will officially no longer be a slave to those hurts and to those emotions – unless you willingly pick these offenses back up and bind yourself with them again.

Crafted Prayer

Father, I am free today. I am no longer a slave to my past or to those who have hurt me. I am Your child, and I know You love me, forgive me, and have a wonderful plan for my life. Thank You for the blood of Christ that covers my sin and provides me forgiveness and holiness in Your eyes.

I have chosen today to forgive, and know that I am completely forgiven for the hurt I have caused You Lord. Help me to walk in my freedom, and not to believe the enemy's lies when they come into my mind regarding those hurtful things in my past. I am not a victim. I am "more than a conqueror in You". I am Your sheep and You know me. You love me completely and there is nothing I have to do to ever win Your love.

Father, would you forgive those people who have hurt me in my past? They need You too, Lord. I pray for their salvation, and that they would come to know you. Would you do a miracle in their lives, and set them free from their pain as well. I choose to bless them today.

Thank You for the grace to walk in freedom today, and every day hereafter.

Notes: *What did you hear God saying to you about forgiveness and freedom?*

_____
_____
_____
_____
_____
_____
_____
_____
_____
_____

DAY 16

Ephesians 6:12 - For we wrestle not against flesh and blood, but against principalities, against powers, against the rulers of the darkness of this world, against spiritual wickedness in high places.

II Corinthians 10:3-5 - For though we walk in the flesh, we do not war according to the flesh, for the weapons of our warfare are not of the flesh, but divinely powerful for the destruction of fortresses. We are destroying speculations and every lofty thing raised up against the knowledge of God, and we are taking every thought captive to the obedience of Christ,

Romans 12:2 - Do not conform any longer to the pattern of this world, but be transformed by the renewing of your mind. Then you will be able to test and approve what God's will is—his good, pleasing and perfect will

Romans 8:5-6 - Those who live according to the sinful nature have their minds set on what that nature desires; but those who live in accordance with the Spirit have their minds set on what the Spirit desires. The mind of sinful man is death, but the mind controlled by the Spirit is life and peace;

It is very obvious in Scripture that we live in a world at war. Our fallen world is ruled by Satan and his minions, and they are not kidding around. Jesus said in John 10:10, "the thief (Satan) comes to steal, kill and destroy". He is out to destroy your life, your marriage, your witness, your kids, and anything else he can. The first verse above confirms that we do indeed "wrestle". Every day we wrestle with our thoughts. Lust, greed, envy, jealousy, failure, hopelessness and anger are only a few of the thoughts that bombard us every day.

What are some of the destructive thoughts you hear on a regular basis? _____
_____
_____

Have you ever felt like a failure? Like you can't measure up? Have you ever felt overwhelmed with guilt or shame from your past sins, or present choices? As we saw yesterday, you can also be enslaved by thoughts of unforgiveness, bitterness and resentment. If so, you have heard and felt the direct attack of your arch enemy.

The second verse confirms for us that we do have weapons at our disposal. Whether we use them or not is up to us! He uses words like "powerful", "destruction" "fortresses", and "captive". The message is clear – war is real, and war is hell. It is serious business and takes serious action on our part. Ignoring it will not make it go away – but, will actually make matters worse.

As a believer, God has given you weapons with which to fight. These weapons are "divinely powerful". They have Divine power in them and they are capable of destroying the fortresses and strongholds in your life, and in the lives of your loved ones. Without them you walk through the battlefield with a pocket knife… weak and vulnerable. With them you are victorious, a destroyer – more than a conqueror. You will discover during these 30 days that these weapons primarily consist of: God's Word, prayer, fasting, thankfulness (praise), praying with another believer, a mind that is being renewed daily in God's Word, speaking God's truth and walking daily in the Spirit.

In what area of your personal or married life do you think the enemy has built a stronghold?_____

Notice in these verses the words "speculations" and "thoughts" – which once again bring you back to the battlefield – your mind. The weapons you use are to help you slay the enemies who continue trying to influence, deceive, manipulate and control your thinking – about God; about yourself; about your marriage, your kids, your friends and your life in general. The path to renewing your mind lies in soaking it in God's truth, and in spending large amounts of time in His presence, praying, listening, and doing battle. You cannot win any other way. You must become a deliberate Christ-follower. You cannot afford to be casual any longer. Casual = Casualty.

How much time daily do you spend reading and meditating on God's Word? _____

How much time do you spend daily communing with God in prayer? _____

Crafted Prayer

Lord, I am desperate for Your presence. I need Your wisdom, Your direction, Your power if I am to make any progress in my life and in my marriage. Help me truly see the seriousness of the war I am living in. Give me the righteous anger with which to fight diligently for my spouse, my marriage and my children. Lives are at stake. Your glory is at stake. Grant me courage as I embark on this journey to know You better, and to learn to follow You. I want to be able to fully trust in Your sovereignty and Your goodness. I know that only in You can I live a victorious life. Would You give me a higher vision and a greater passion to do whatever it takes to defeat the enemies in my life and in my marriage? Thank You.

Notes: *What did you hear God saying to you about your personal spiritual warfare?*

_____
_____
_____
_____
_____
_____

> **When a Christian shuns fellowship with other Christians, the devil smiles. When he stops studying the Bible, the devil laughs. When he stops praying, the devil shouts for joy.**
> **~ Corrie ten Boom**

DAY 17

Proverbs 4:23 - *Above all else, guard your heart, for it is the wellspring of life.*

Philippians 4:7 - *And the peace of God, which surpasses all comprehension, will guard your hearts and your minds in Christ Jesus.*

After yesterday's discussion on the spiritual battle we are in, let's look at some additional verses about the battlefield – the theater where the daily conflict is fought – our heart (mind).

"Above ALL else" is a very bold statement. Above everything else, you are to guard your heart. Not your literal heart, but your spiritual heart – your mind. Only you can control the things you let into your mind. You control the remote control, the radio dial and the computer mouse. What you choose to look at and listen to will greatly influence the battle underway to destroy your life. As a Christian, you must diligently guard your mind from the relentless assault of the enemy. No one else can do it for you. You can't pray and ask God to do it for you – it is your responsibility to "guard".

What are two things that come to mind that you need to do a better job of guarding your heart from?

1. _____
2. _____

You do have some help in the guarding process however. The second verse tells us that God's peace will guard your heart also. God is a God of peace. Peace is a by-product of living in God's presence. For most of us, peace is the absence of conflict, or noise, or hustle and bustle. God says "He is peace". If we are in His presence – we experience peace. If we are far from His presence, we experience "not-peace" → anxiety, fear, etc.

God's peace is something far beyond our comprehension. When you experience it, you know it. Ask someone who has felt His peace and presence after a loved one has died, or when they were dealing with a critical illness or rebellious teenager at home. They can't really explain it – it's just there, and it's tangible. It is not made up, it is real, and present – they can feel it.

In your hectic world today, experiencing some real peace would feel pretty good wouldn't it? You are physically tired and emotionally spent most of the time. Life comes at you like a fast-moving train. You can't stop it, and there is little to even slow it down. Your marriage relationship seems to consist of solving endless problems. Kids, drama, in-laws, work, finances, debt, health, schedules, - you name it. Your mind is overloaded with thoughts, issues, demands for solutions, deadlines, schedules, temptations, and more. Where is an oasis in the midst of all this noise? **God.**

Not the mean, lightening bolt throwing God of your old mythology book. Not the scary Wizard-of-Oz God - but Father God. A Person, a real and present God, Who loves you and longs to spend time with you. A Father who hugs, who kisses, who restores and lavishes blessings upon His children.

This God loves you more than anyone you know. His love is not conditional on your performance. He knows all about your past sin and still there is nothing you can do to make Him love you less, and nothing you can do to make Him love you more. He simply loves you – yes, YOU.

As you draw near to this God you will experience a peace like no other. He says "come unto me all you who are weary and weighed down with life, and I WILL give you rest" (**Matt. 11:28**). As a perfect Shepherd, He is always leading you to green grass, and still waters – so your soul can be refreshed. He is always protecting you and comforting you when you are weary or hurting. See for yourself what He will do if you just draw near to Him.

Write down two areas in your life where you really need to find some rest.

1. _____ 2. _____

If you are not experiencing peace in your heart/soul, then stop and turn to Him. In the same way you take a break from work and busyness to go to the beach or the mountains for a vacation, you need to get away from the hustle and bustle of life, and the noise resounding in your mind – and get alone with the God of peace. You will find great rest, comfort and healing there.

As you choose to turn away from the temptations of this world, turn to Him. Spend time with Him. Psalm 23 tells us that He will lead you to "still waters" and "green pastures". He can't wait to meet with you, and to bless you.

Crafted Prayer

Father, thank you again for Your love for me. Thank you for giving me peace, and rest within the storms of life. Would you show me how to carve out more time to spend with You, just basking in Your presence? I want to experience more of You. I want to feel Your presence in my marriage, I want to embrace Your joy and approach life with peace knowing You are with me and You care about every aspect, big and small, of my life. Thank you for my marriage. Help us experience more of Your life together as we seek You in our home.

Lord, help me to do a better job of guarding my heart. Help me be more discerning about the influences I allow in my mind and heart. I need You to remind me daily to protect my eyes and ears from evil influences and to be diligent in my responsibility to also protect my wife and family.

Notes: *What did you hear God saying to you about guarding your heart and drawing near to Him?*

DAY 18

Ephesians 5:15-21 - Therefore be careful how you walk, not as unwise men but as wise, making the most of your time, because the days are evil. So then do not be foolish, but understand what the will of the Lord is. And do not get drunk with wine, for that is dissipation, but be filled with the Spirit, speaking to one another in psalms and hymns and spiritual songs, singing and making melody with your heart to the Lord; always giving thanks for all things in the name of our Lord Jesus Christ to God, even the Father; and be subject to one another in the fear of Christ.

Are you careful how you walk? Are you making the most of your time? Are you being continually filled with God's Spirit? Are you continually giving thanks in all things? Are you walking in submission to the needs of your spouse? I didn't say it – God did.

Again – the goal is progress, not perfection. None of us is perfect at this. But these Words from the heart of God pierce deep into our soul and convict us about the choices we make every single day. Spend time today asking God to show you what each of these means in your life, and how to better live the kind of life He calls you to live.

Be careful how you live – You need to be diligent and purposeful about your daily walk with Jesus, or hours will turn into days, days will turn into weeks, weeks to months, and before you know it an entire year, or an entire decade will fly by and you will have missed out. "Someday I will spend more time with my kids." "Someday I will have more time with my wife". "As soon as I find the right church I will get serious with God". There are thousands of excuses people use to put off doing what they know they should do. Don't fall for it. Don't be deceived. Life is indeed short, and life is precious. You only get one chance at it – and you need to "be careful" to live each day.

The days are evil. It seems like this year is darker than last. The world is growing darker. Sin is abounding more and more. Yet, God is still on the throne. He is still in charge. He has a master plan, a loving, wonderful plan for each of our lives. He can be trusted. You must be careful not to be sucked in to the whirlpool of life that wants to drag you down and choke off your mission, your joy, your life.

Be filled with the Spirit. The verse actually says – "Be being filled" or keep being filled – continuously. This doesn't happen automatically. You must choose to ask, to seek and desire to be filled by Him and for Him to empower you to produce abundant fruit in your life.

Giving thanks – in all things. It doesn't say "for" all things, but with God's help, you can live a life of thankfulness "in" all things. Life is hard, and you can learn to be thankful for God's love, His sovereign plan for your life, His continual presence with you, and His abundance of riches that are available to you

Name two ways you could be more "careful" about how you are living right now:

1. _____
2. _____

On most days, do you feel like you live a life "filled" with the Spirit? _____

What would living that way look like to you, and those around you?
_____
_____

How would your relationship with your wife change if you were more deliberate about asking God to fill you with His Spirit every day? _____
_____
_____
_____

What are the things you are most thankful for in your life today?
_____
_____
_____
_____

In what areas of your marriage should you be more thankful?
_____
_____
_____
_____

Crafted Prayer

Father, speak to me about this passage. Show me how to live this way, and how to be more thankful, more deliberate, more careful, and how to continue to be filled with Your Spirit every day. I pray You would even give me the "want to" on those days I really don't.

Help me know that my life and my marriage matter. Time is precious. I need to get serious about what really matters. I want my life to count and I know that only You can lead me and make my years here worth something. Speak to me about what matters most to You, and to my wife and family. Forgive me for being lazy and basically apathetic about living life in this way. I have been self-focused and only concerned with my agenda, my goals and my dreams.

Help me to more deliberately pursue the things that matter most. Show me Your heart for me and lead me into the "good plans" You have for me. Thank You for forgiving me and helping me start afresh today.

Notes: *What did you hear God saying to you about walking more carefully and being filled with His Spirit?*

_____
_____
_____
_____
_____
_____
_____
_____
_____
_____
_____
_____
_____

> **"A heart not satisfied by Christ, will always be a discontented heart"**

DAY 19

Galatians 5:16 - *But I say, walk by the Spirit, and you will not carry out the desire of the flesh.*

Galatians 5:25 - *If we live by the Spirit, let us also walk by the Spirit.*

According to Galatians 5, the desires of the flesh include: sexual immorality, impurity, lustful pleasures, idolatry, sorcery, hostility, quarreling, jealousy, outbursts of anger, selfish ambition, dissension, division, envy, drunkenness, wild parties, and other sins like these. In Ephesians, Paul adds: filthiness, silly talk, coarse jesting, and covetousness to the list. There are countless other deeds unlisted, but these are enough for us to get the message.

If you don't walk in the Spirit, your life is going to be filled with lousy things. If your life is filled with lousy things – you're probably not walking in the Spirit.

What do you think about when you hear the word "walking"? Walking involves effort; it speaks of moving forward; it denotes progress. You cannot walk standing still. You can't walk without effort. There is no neutral involved in walking. You must exert energy to put one foot in front of the other. Walking takes you from one place to another place.

So, walking *in* the Spirit, or *with* the Spirit must mean something similar. You make progress, you move forward, you go from one place to another – with the Spirit. You walk alongside, or together with the Spirit of God. The Book of John tells us that you have the Spirit "in" you. So, wherever you go, you take the Spirit along. Walking with (inline with), or *in the Spirit*

means to walk under the influence and unction of the Spirit of God. In order to do that, you have to ask where He wants you to go, when and how. Then (and this is the hardest part) you have to be willing to follow – to walk *with* Him - not ahead of Him. You don't make your own decisions about where and how to walk and then just ask the Spirit to "be with you" and "bless you".

If you are mentally in tune with the Spirit – your actions will also get in step with the Spirit. If you are listening to His voice, and obey what He says, He will lead you in "straight paths". If you are struggling with issues like lust, anger, fear, defeat, pornography, gluttony, despair, greed, jealousy, etc. – the quickest path to wholeness is to learn to "walk" in the Spirit. This promise says that if you do that – you will not carry out those deeds of the flesh. Which path will you choose? Every day, and sometimes several times a day, you have to choose to walk toward or away from the Spirit and life of God. Pray for strength to choose wisely.

What issue(s) from the list above do you struggle with most?
_____

Whenever you find yourself struggling with thoughts and/or actions in these areas, do what Jesus did (not Eve) when He was tempted. Don't dwell on/ponder/contemplate/entertain it – rebuke it. Just stop and pray <u>out loud</u> (Satan cannot hear your thoughts) a simple prayer like this:

Father, right now I am struggling with feelings of _____. I know they are not from You and are not appropriate. Would You help me right now? Would You free me from bondage to these thoughts and temptations, and help me to focus on You and Your Word? I resist you Satan and all forces of darkness, in the name of Jesus Christ, and by His power and His authority, I command you to leave my presence and my thoughts. I am free in Christ and not bound by your schemes. Depart from me right now, in Jesus' name.

James 4:7 says, "Submit therefore unto God. Resist the devil and he WILL flee from you."

It doesn't say, he "might" flee. He **will** flee because; a) the name of Jesus has authority over him, b) as a Christian and a child of the King, you have authority over him and all his schemes and devices, and c) God said so in His Word. So believe it, speak it, and walk away from those things that bind you and make your life miserable. – today.

After you pray, you need to immediately start walking in the Spirit, by reading His Word, speaking His Word, singing worship songs, or even continuing to pray and express your thankfulness for victory over what was harassing you. Here are a few Scriptures that you should be familiar with:

> **2 Corinthians 10:3-5**
> *For though we live in the world, **we** do not **wage war** as the world does. The weapons **we fight with** are not the weapons of the world. On the contrary, they have **divine power to demolish strongholds**. **We demolish** arguments and every pretension that sets itself up against the knowledge of God, and **we take captive** every thought to make it obedient to Christ.*

> **Romans 8:37-40**
> *No, in all these things we are **more than conquerors** through him who loved us. For I am convinced that neither death nor life, neither angels nor demons, neither the present nor the future, nor any powers, neither height nor depth, nor anything else in all creation, will be able to separate us from the love of God that is in Christ Jesus our Lord.*

Crafted Prayer

Father, I really need your help in this area. I want to learn how to walk in the Spirit and not fulfill the lusts of my flesh. I keep trying, but failing. I can't do this on my own, but I know with Your help I can live a life of freedom. Please fill me anew with the power of Your Spirit. Give me the desire to choose the best path, and to continually fix my gaze on You. Help me stay in Your Word and soak my mind in the Truth of it.

Thank you for the authority You have given me over the enemy and over all of his schemes. Grant me the desire to break free from the bondage to these sins that entangle me, and to experience the freedom I now have as Your child. Help me live a life on continual conversation with You, and train my spiritual ears to hear Your still small voice. Speak loudly to me Lord. Help me walk with You today and experience the abundant joy and freedom in Your presence.

Notes: *What did you hear God saying to you about walking in the Spirit and using your spiritual authority?*

_____
_____
_____
_____
_____
_____
_____
_____
_____
_____
_____

DAY 20

Galatians 5:22-23 - But the fruit of the Spirit is love, joy, peace, patience, kindness, goodness, faithfulness, gentleness, self-control; against such things there is no law

Yesterday you took a look at the desires of your flesh. Today, God shows you what a person looks like who is walking in the Spirit. There are fruits that are evident to those around him. Remember Day 11? In that lesson we clearly saw that we can do nothing on our own. You are a branch – not the vine. If you don't stay connected to Him, you will not produce fruit in your life or marriage.

Evidence that you are truly walking with God is that you will have fruit hanging off of your life. Others will see the love, kindness, goodness, etc. that you show to others and how you respond to life's circumstances with joy, patience and the faith that God is good and He knows what He is doing. You can't make this stuff up. You can't fake your way through a consistent life with this kind of fruit.

What do others see when they look at your marriage? Do they say, "Wow", he treats his wife with such love, kindness and patience"? Do they see your self-control when facing difficult issues, or your complete trust in God when life turns South on you?

What do you think people say when they observe your relationship with your wife today? _____

Problem is – these fruits don't grow naturally or automatically in your life. You may naturally be an optimist, or a gentle person, but to live a life filled with abundant spiritual fruit takes supernatural help. You need to attach yourself to a vine that is flowing with rich, life-giving sap that will nourish you and produce lasting fruit.

A life that exhibits this kind of fruitfulness is a life that brings glory to God. People are drawn to people like these. People seek out people like these and ask them "how do you do it?" God provides the fruit, and then He provides the opportunities to tell other people about the Vine. What a great God we have.

What kind of fruit would you like for God to produce in your life?
_____
_____
_____

If you don't see these fruits growing in your life on a regular basis, or don't see even any buds on the branches – then now is the time to get back in touch with the Vine. If you have pulled away from your life source, and walked for a while as a dry branch – He is eager to have you grafted back into Him. Don't put it off any longer.

> **"Abide in Me, and I in you. As the branch cannot bear fruit of itself unless it abides in the vine, so neither can you unless you abide in Me." ~John 15:4**

Remember – if you ever experience the opposite of these fruits in your marriage, ie: despair and sadness instead of joy; anxiety and fear instead of peace; impatience instead of patience; harshness and anger instead of kindness, etc. – know that you are tasting the fruits of the flesh. This means you are not experiencing the fruits of the Spirit, and it is time to take action.

On Days 16 and 17 we read about our sworn enemy and the constant war that rages around us and in us. We also read about the necessity to fight with spiritual weapons and to guard our heart at all cost. One of the first signs that you are under attack personally, or in your marriage, is when you recognize these fruits of the flesh and not the fruits of the Spirit. It also means that one, or both of you, are not walking in the Spirit and guarding your heart. This is the time to immediately STOP, get together with your wife, and pray.

Pray against the forces of darkness that are attacking you, your wife and your marriage. Pray for God's presence to fill your hearts and your home. Ask the Holy Spirit to show you anything you need to repent (change your mind) of, ask God and your wife to forgive you if need be, and then get back up again. Shake off the "dust" of the battle and thank God for a fresh start.

Crafted Prayer

Father, thank You that no matter where I am in my relationship with You right now – I can always come back to You. If I have walked away from the Vine and lived life on my own terms – I apologize. I want to come back and attach to You. I am desperate for Your life flowing in and through me again. Thank You that You love me, accept me, and are eager to forgive me and lead me once again.

Show me any area where I may have hurt my wife with my words or my actions, and give me the courage to say I am sorry. Help me to do better, Lord. Please fill my life with fruit again, and help me love my wife as You have loved me. Let Your fruit be evident in my life and in our marriage, Lord. I can't do this without You.

Notes: *What did you hear God saying to you about the fruit in your life and your marriage?*

_____
_____
_____
_____
_____
_____
_____

Marriage is our last, best chance to grow up
~ Joseph Barth

DAY 21

Philippians 2:3 - *Do nothing from selfishness or empty conceit, but with humility of mind regard one another as more important than yourselves;*

"Do nothing" that is selfish, sounds like a pretty impossible task doesn't it? Here is yet another verse that calls us to do something we are incapable of doing. How are we expected to live up to such a standard?

As we have already discussed, you can't. You are helpless to live up to such a standard without the direct and continuous intervention from God, through His Holy Spirit. Unless you choose to walk by His Spirit, you are doomed to continue on your natural, self-seeking path through life. You see, you are born with your "default switch" set to "me".

From birth our natural bent is toward those things which make "me" happy and fulfill "me".

List two areas in your life where you automatically default to what "you" want?

1. _____
2. _____

Some of a child's first words are "mine", and "I want". Sadly, most adults never seem to kick the habit either. Marriage has a way of bringing out your deep-seeded desire to please #1 – you.

Once again, Jesus is our supreme example: (**Philippians 2:5-8**)

Have this attitude in yourselves which was also in Christ Jesus, who, although He existed in the form of God, did not regard equality with God a thing to be grasped, but emptied Himself, taking the form of a bond-servant, and being made in the likeness of men. Being found in appearance as a man, He humbled Himself by becoming obedient to the point of death, even death on a cross.

Jesus humbled himself and voluntarily left His throne in heaven to become a mortal man, who obeyed God even though it cost His life. He lovingly laid down His life so that you and I can live, both now and for eternity. He chose to come here. He chose to obey God. He chose to forgive those who tortured him. He is our supreme example of what unselfishness, humility and putting others first look like.

What do you think Paul meant when he used the phrase "with humility of mind" in the verse for today? _____
_____

**None are so empty as those who are full of themselves.
Benjamin Whichcote**

If you were being completely honest, do you regard your wife as *more important than yourself?*

Think of three ways you could lay down your life for your wife:

1. _____
2. _____
3. _____

Crafted Prayer

Father, You surely know that I am a selfish person. I instinctively do those things that make me look good, or that please me in some way. Even though I want to be more unselfish, I find that I easily slip back into a "me" focus without any effort at all.

Would You do a profound work in my heart? Would You change me and allow me to become more like Jesus, and put others (especially my wife) ahead of myself? I know I can't do that in my own strength and I am asking You right now for more power to live like that. I know that it is only by Your power and grace that I can ever do anything that is truly others-focused.

Lord, show me tangible ways that I can begin to put the needs/desires/dreams of my wife ahead of my own. Show me where I have hurt her, frustrated her or stifled her in any way.

Help me to walk with You today. I want to hear Your voice and follow where You lead me. I know as I abide in You and stay close to You, that You will lead me and make me into the man and the husband You designed me to be. I am desperate for You. I offer You my life and am excited about what is ahead Lord.

Notes: *What did you hear God saying to you about your default setting of selfishness?*

_____
_____
_____
_____
_____
_____

> **I believe the first test of a truly great man is his humility. I do not mean by humility, doubt of his own powers. But really great men have a curious feeling that the greatness is not in them, but through them. And they see something divine in every other man. ~ John Ruskin**

DAY 22

Ephesians 4:29-32 - Let no unwholesome word proceed from your mouth, but only such a word as is good for edification according to the need of the moment, so that it will give grace to those who hear. Do not grieve the Holy Spirit of God, by whom you were sealed for the day of redemption. Let all bitterness and wrath and anger and clamor and slander be put away from you, along with all malice. Be kind to one another, tender-hearted, forgiving each other, just as God in Christ also has forgiven you.

It doesn't get much clearer than this. "Let no", "do not", "Be" – are pretty forceful words directed at us from God regarding our relationships. These are also commands from the heart of God – not holy suggestions for our consideration.

Do you see any of these present in your marriage today? - unwholesome words, non-edifying hurtful words, bitterness, wrath, anger (spoken or unspoken), resentment, slander, unkindness, stubbornness or unforgiveness.

If so, there is some major "clean-up" needed. We all slip up and say things we don't mean or things we wish we hadn't said. None of us does it perfectly. But the question is – do you see a pattern of behavior, or words used in conversation, that are not healthy and even sinful?

Which kind of words do you struggle with most? _____
_____

List some "unwholesome words" you have used in conversation with your wife in the past. _____
_____
_____

List some words that you could use that would be edifying and full of grace to your wife? _____
_____
_____

Listen to what God says about the importance of the words we use:

> **Proverbs 18:21** - *Words kill, words give life; they're either poison or fruit—you choose.*
>
> **Proverbs 12:18** - *Reckless words pierce like a sword, but the tongue of the wise brings healing.*
>
> **Proverbs 16:24** - *Pleasant words are a honeycomb, sweet to the soul and healing to the bones.*
>
> **Proverbs 21:23** - *He who guards his mouth and his tongue keeps himself from calamity.*

If you truly want healing in your marriage, and to restore oneness with your wife, you have to decide to deal with this issue today. It's time to get with God and bring this all to Him. He's not mad. He's not distant. He's not out to get you. He is sad, that your relationship with your wife has gotten to this point, but He is longing to help you get back where you want to be. He has all the power you need, all the wisdom you long for, and all the forgiveness to help you make a fresh start, and change your behavior.

Action Step: Take some time and start with the prayer below. Afterwards, get with your wife and ask her to forgive you for any hurtful and harsh words you have said to her. Don't put any conditions on it, like: "as soon as you……", or "if you… then I will….". You need to take responsibility for what you have

done, what you have said, and the consequences of those actions. This is a major step toward healing, so don't hurry through it. It is hard to do, but God will honor you for doing it.

Whether your wife forgives you, or apologizes for her actions, is totally up to God and is not your responsibility. You have to trust that to God. You are responsible before God for your actions/words and the hurt they have caused.

If you ever hear these types of words again, you need to immediately stop and check your spiritual barometer. Am I walking with God? Am I listening to the enemy? Am I guarding my heart? Do I need to ask forgiveness?

Crafted Prayer

Father, You know me better than anyone and you know I am far from perfect. Would You forgive me for hurting my wife by acting in an unholy manner? Forgive me for grieving Your heart and damaging the marriage relationship that You designed for my fulfillment and for Your glory. Give me the courage and strength to ask my wife for forgiveness and to take responsibility for my poor choices.

Help me to think before I speak. Help me not to react when I am hurt or irritated. Cleanse my heart afresh today. Help me speak to my wife as if she was Your daughter and priceless treasure — because she is. Make me keenly aware of my thoughts and the words that come from my lips before I speak them. Holy Spirit lead me and teach me how to be a kinder husband.

Notes: *What did you hear God saying to you about the words you speak to your wife?*

_____
_____
_____
_____
_____
_____
_____

_____
_____
_____
_____
_____

"The real art of conversation is not only to say the right thing at the right time, but to leave unsaid the wrong thing at the tempting moment." ~ Dorothy Nevill

DAY 23

I Corinthians 7:3-5 - *The husband should fulfill his marital duty to his wife, and likewise the wife to her husband. The wife's body does not belong to her alone but also to her husband. In the same way, the husband's body does not belong to him alone but also to his wife. Do not deprive each other except by mutual consent and for a time, so that you may devote yourselves to prayer. Then come together again so that Satan will not tempt you because of your lack of self-control.*

Another translation puts it this way - *The marriage bed must be a place of mutuality—the husband seeking to satisfy his wife, the wife seeking to satisfy her husband. Marriage is not a place to "stand up for your rights." Marriage is a decision to serve the other, whether in bed or out.*

As we have seen several times during this Challenge, the key ingredient necessary for success in this area is also – unselfishness. Sexual intimacy is all about pleasing your wife. You will receive plenty of pleasure if you do a great job of pleasing her.

"Women need a reason for sex, men just need a place."
~ Billy Crystal

Your wife needs more than the act of sex to enjoy intimacy. She needs to feel loved and appreciated. She wants to feel attractive and desired by you. She is wired differently and that is by God's design. Embrace her differences and her unique needs. It is in meeting them that you will also meet your own and experience greater intimacy and oneness.

Your wife is also more relational. She typically is thinking about dozens of issues, chores, people and their circumstances at any given time. She is concerned about her parents, the kids, the neighbors, the people in your small group, the people she works with, her relatives, etc. Unlike you, she can't just turn off her thoughts and concerns and dive into some romantic sexual episode. She needs to be romanced. She needs a reason to turn off the switches in her brain that keep her pre-occupied with the needs of everyone in her sphere of life. This is where you come in ....

What do you call it when a husband washes the dishes, or vacuums the floor? Foreplay.

Demonstrating to your wife that you care about her and want to lighten her load around the house is romantic to her. Sending her a text or email during the day to just say 'hi, I'm thinking about you" also tells her she is special to you. Your wife still needs to be courted, romanced and wooed.

Write down three things you can do to romance your wife and show her she is special.

1. _____
2. _____
3. _____

Once again, the Bible is clear that you don't wait until your wife does a better job, or understands your sexual needs, or anything else – before you do what He says to do. Just begin to do it, and trust Him to bless you and to speak to her.

There are four things that you also must know that will stifle, or kill your sexual intimacy:

1. **Not feeling loved** - it doesn't matter how long you have been together, or how often you have told her, done nice things for her or given her gifts. It doesn't matter how well you have provided for her. What she remains insecure about, nearly every day, is "do you really love me?" She needs very frequent, and very sincere reassurance. Your actions will speak much more to her than your words.

2. **Fatigue** – far too many couples have nothing left for each other at the end of their hectic days. They are exhausted mentally and physically.

3. **Unresolved Conflict or Issues** – because your wife is wired to be more relational, she will more easily remember harsh words, or unloving actions for a longer period of time. She feels the disconnect when the two of you have not resolved your latest disagreement or still harbor unresolved anger or hurt.

4. **Poor Self Esteem and Body Image** – the majority of women in America are insecure with their bodies and their self esteem. They truly feel inferior to those who look better, or do things better than they do. They desperately need to know that you still find them attractive and desirable, and that they please you sexually.

Men may think about some of these issues, but can instantly turn them off and enjoy sex. Not so with your wife. It is up to you to take the lead to 1) help reduce her stress and work load, b) apologize and work to resolve any outstanding conflicts or issues between you, and c) vocalize your physical attraction and desire for your wife. **Remember** – your wife needs to feel connected with you emotionally before she has any desire for physical connection.

Crafted Prayer

Father, thank You for creating sexual intimacy as a means of experiencing oneness and connection with my wife. Forgive me again for being selfish in this area. You know my needs, and what I struggle with. I want to be more unselfish and giving in this area, but it is hard to do without for very long.

Would You remind me often to demonstrate my love for her by the things I say and do? Give me the courage to choose being with her over other selfish pursuits, so she will know that she is more important than my work, friends and hobbies. Help me love her better, Lord.

Help me to take the lead in our marriage to make sure we don't have unresolved conflicts or harbor any hurt feelings toward each other. Give me the courage to be the first to apologize and ask for forgiveness when I say or do anything unloving. I really do want to be the best husband I can be, and to love my wife as You love the church. Show me how to love her and serve her better, and how to make her feel my love for her and my attraction to her.

Notes: *What did you hear God saying to you about your role in experiencing sexual intimacy with your wife?*

_____
_____
_____
_____
_____
_____
_____
_____
_____
_____
_____
_____
_____

DAY 24

II Corinthians 9:6-7 - *Now this I say, he who sows sparingly will also reap sparingly, and he who sows bountifully will also reap bountifully. Each one must do just as he has purposed in his heart, not grudgingly or under compulsion, for God loves a cheerful giver.*

Galatians 6:7 - *Do not be deceived, God is not mocked; for whatever a man sows, this he will also reap.*

You have already seen that you cannot do "anything" without Christ. It is not about praying one-time prayer, but a daily, moment-by-moment walk with the Good Shepherd. This verse is a strong reminder that you get out of your relationships what you put into them – your relationship with God, and your relationship with your wife. If you spend very little time with Him in prayer, you will hear very little from Him. If you don't take the time to draw near to Him, you shouldn't expect Him to draw near to you. If you turn your back on Him and deliberately live your life in disobedience (sin) – He will always be with you, but cannot bless your efforts.

The same is true in your marriage. If you invest little in trying to understand your wife, you will continue to scratch your head in wonder. If you spend little time with her, your affection and attraction will grow stiff and cold. If you allow deceptive thoughts to influence your mind and beliefs – you will react with unkind and hurtful words. If you don't renew your mind with God's Word daily, you will begin to slowly drift away from Him and from your spouse. If you choose not to walk in the Spirit, you should not expect to see any of the fruits of the Spirit in your life, or in your marriage. You get to decide.

One a scale of 1-10, where would you rank yourself on the amount of time you spend with Jesus every day?

(none) 1 2 3 4 5 6 7 8 9 10 (over 1 hour)

One a scale of 1-10, where would you rank yourself on the amount of time you spend interacting with your wife every day?

(none) 1 2 3 4 5 6 7 8 9 10 (over 1 hour)

Fortunately, the opposite is also true. The more time you invest with your wife, the more you grow to love and appreciate her. The more time you spend in God's presence, the more your life is forever changed into His likeness. The more you seek Him and His will for your life, the more things seem to "work out" and the better decisions you seem to make.

You really do reap what you sow in these two areas. If you want a bountiful walk with Jesus – you simply have to sow bountifully by spending time with Him. The same is true for marriage. The more you really seek God's heart and blessing for your relationship – the better it becomes. Even if you don't feel like it – God will richly bless you for obeying what He says. He always does what He says He will do.

> **We are in danger of forgetting that we cannot do what God does, and that God will not do what we can do**
> **~ Oswald Chambers**

God loves a cheerful giver. The more you give Him your life, your marriage, your agenda, your will, etc. – the more He loves to give back to you. He says He will give "above and beyond all you can ask or even think". That's amazing. The more you give your time and heart to your wife – the more she will respond with love and respect for you.

As the head of your household, God calls you to be the initiator of His will. His will is for peace, harmony and oneness in your home.

Remember – your marriage is the showcase where the world can see Christ's love for His bride, the church. Your marriage matters to God and is supposed to bring Him glory. It is not about your happiness. That will come as a byproduct of seeking to glorify Him.

How would you describe the difference between Christ being your Savior, and Him being your Lord? _____
_____
_____

What areas of your life do you find the most difficulty giving over to the Lordship of Christ? (finances, work, hobbies, free time, marriage, children, health, sex life, thought life, etc.)_____
_____
_____

Crafted Prayer

Father, forgive me for being stingy with You. I have held back my time, talent and resources from You knowing full well that it is You Who provides them to me in the first place. Forgive me also for holding back with my wife. Help me be a willing and cheerful giver – of my love, time and whatever else is needed to make our marriage awesome. I want to sow bountifully with You, and with my wife – and trust You to produce a bountiful "crop" in my life.

Lord, show me areas in my life that I need to turn over control to You. I want You to be Lord of my life as well as Savior. Forgive my reluctance to let go of things I have held on to for so long. Help me to trust Your goodness and Your sovereignty. You are a generous and loving Father, and I know I can trust You with everything in my life. Lead me as I seek to know and trust You more.

Notes: *What did you hear God saying to you about sowing and reaping in your relationship with Him and with your wife?*
_____
_____
_____

_____
_____
_____
_____
_____
_____
_____

> "Give, and you will receive. Your gift will return to you in full—pressed down, shaken together to make room for more, running over, and poured into your lap. The amount you give will determine the amount you get back." ~ Luke 6:38

DAY 25

Matthew 6:20-21 - *But store up for yourselves treasures in heaven, where neither moth nor rust destroys, and where thieves do not break in and steal; for where your treasure is, there your heart will be also.*

What would you say are your most valuable possessions?

___

God is perfectly okay with you having possessions. In fact, He wants to bless your hard work, and your obedience. You are not promised wealth or possessions in this life, but God is certainly capable of blessing you in that way. You probably know many Christian people who have many possessions, and many who don't have much.

> **"The Lord makes poor and rich;**
> **He brings low, He also exalts." ~ 1 Samuel 2:7**

Whether God blesses you with material wealth or not is not the point. You can have very little and still live your life focused on material things and not on God's glory. This too, is a matter of the heart. As the verse says, it is where your heart is (your focus, your desires, your motives) that really matters. God says in Matthew 6:24, that "you cannot serve two masters – God and money". The first of the Ten Commandments is that you will have "no other God before Him". Money, whether you have little or much, can easily become your God.

Do you measure your worth by the things you possess, or don't possess? Men instinctively seem to measure another man by what he does for a living, the kind of car he drives or the house he lives in. There is something deep inside that pushes us forward to achieve more, accomplish more, and to get more. It is time to take a step back and ask yourself, and God, where your treasure really lies.

If you are being honest, what would you say is something you would like to have or achieve that could easily become a "god" in your life? _____

Switching gears, let's look inside your marriage. The second part of the verse above says that wherever our treasure is, your heart will be there also. Regarding your marriage, where is your heart right now? _____
_____

As we have already seen, your wife is a treasure, hand-crafted by God Himself, specifically for you. She, above any other woman on the planet, is designed for you as your "essential helper" and completer. She is the rest of you. She is also a daughter of God who He loves very much. She is His treasure, and He expects her to be treated as such.

If you find that your heart has wandered away from your wife and that you don't have the same feelings you once had for her – you need to take some time and check your heart. If she is not your #1 earthly treasure, your heart will not be completely hers. You can pray the crafted prayer below and ask God to change your heart, but you also need to choose every day to love her and treat her as the precious helper she is.

What are three things about your wife that you treasure?
1. _____
2. _____
3. _____

Silent gratitude isn't much use to anyone. ~G.B. Stern

If the only prayer you said in your whole life was, "thank you," that would suffice. ~Meister Eckhart

You must learn to live with an attitude of gratitude. Every good thing you have is from the Lord. He is worthy of our thanks. You will be amazed by the results in your life and in your marriage if you will wake up every day and begin to thank God for your wife and all that He is doing in your life.

Crafted Prayer

Father, I am truly thankful for everything You have done, and are doing in my life. I know that You created my wife just for me and that You are using her in my life to make me a better man and conform me into Your image. Help me be more mindful, and more thankful, for that.

Lord, would You do a work in my heart to develop a genuine attitude of thankfulness for Your plans for me, and especially for my wife? Help me to see her as Your precious gift and help me to make her my #1 treasure in life. I want my heart to be with her. I want her to be my greatest treasure and our marriage to radiate with Your glory. You know I can't do anything by myself, so please fill me with Your Spirit and lead me each and every day as I draw near to You.

Notes: *What did you hear God saying to you about your heart and your treasure?*

_____
_____
_____
_____
_____

"Feeling gratitude and not expressing it is like wrapping a present and not giving it."
~ William Arthur Ward

DAY 26

Ecclesiastes 4:9 - *Two people are better off than one, for they can help each other succeed.*

Ecclesiastes 4:12 - *A person standing alone can be attacked and defeated, but two can stand back-to-back and conquer.*

> **"You must learn from the mistakes of others. You can't possibly live long enough to make them all yourself."**
> **~ Sam Levenson**

In just three decades, between 1960 and 1990, the percentage of children living apart from their biological fathers more than doubled, from 17 percent to 36 percent. Today over 50 percent of American children are going to sleep each evening without being able to say good night to their dads.

So, who do you talk to about life's hard issues? Most men have no one. We have buddies but rarely do we talk about temptation, lust, pornography, addiction, intimacy issues with the wife, job fears, etc. Most of us typically ignore them or sweep them under the nearest rug and hope they go away. They don't.

What do you think Henry David Thoreau meant when he penned one of his most famous quotes – "Most men lead lives of quiet desperation"? _____

_____

Because of our innate ability to "suck it up" and "gut it out", we tend to internalize problems and issues. That could explain why men typically die sooner than women. The verses above tell us very plainly that life, and warfare, work better when you have a buddy, a comrade or mentor to walk with you.

A mentor is one who serves as a teacher or model and often provides individualized instruction and encouragement. A mentor is "*a brain to pick, an ear to listen, and a push in the right direction*," according to the Uncommon Individual Foundation, an organization devoted to mentoring research and training. It reports that mentoring is one of the most powerful tools we have for influencing human behavior.

Think about it – How did you learn most of the things that you know? You were taught by someone else. Someone taught you simple tasks like brushing your teeth or writing your name. Others came along and taught you more complex tasks and skills, like multiplication, or how to throw a baseball. We have all had others in our lives who have mentored us along the way.

Mentoring has been around for centuries. Early tradesmen, craftsmen and farmers learned their skills from their parents and grandparents, or from others in their town or region. Artists, musicians and educators honed their natural gifting at the feet of mentors. Mentors have been responsible for shaping not only physical skills, but also individual knowledge, technique and attitude.

The Bible is full with examples of mentoring: Eli and Samuel, Elijah and Elisha, Moses and Joshua, Naomi and Ruth, Barnabas and Paul, Paul and Timothy. And, of course, Jesus and the disciples are a great example of mentoring.

Moses and Joshua
(Exodus, Numbers, Joshua 1)
Eli and Samuel (1 Sam 1-3)
Elijah and Elisha (I Kings 19)
Naomi and Ruth (Ruth 1)
Paul and Barnabas (Acts 13-15)
Paul and Timothy
(Acts 16, 1 Tim 4 and 6)

Finding a mentor may be one of the smartest decisions you will make regarding your life and your marriage. Someone older and more experienced can offer great wisdom and help you avoid many landmines that are in your path. Where else do you learn how life and marriage work? Left to figure it out on your own (our natural inclination) you are left to learn by trial and error. As you know already, this can be a very painful teaching technique.

How do you go about approaching a mentor? First, make a list of three men who you think exemplify the kind of life and marriage you would like to have.

1. _____
2. _____
3. _____

Pray for wisdom as you consider how to approach them, and pray also for God to prepare the right person's heart. God will provide an opportunity for you to approach them where it is not awkward or weird. Simply ask each of them, one at a time, if he would be available to have coffee, breakfast or lunch sometime, and tell him you have something you would like to talk with him about. You both will know if you are a "fit" after that initial meeting. You will have peace and confirmation from God, or you will feel like it was nothing more than a meeting with a nice man. Let Him lead you.

Crafted Prayer

Father, I know that it is not good for me to live life on my own. I need another man in my life to encourage, admonish and challenge me. I also need another man who understands what I am going through, and how to counsel me and fight alongside me in prayer.

Lord, You are the ultimate mentor. You are the primary person I need to stay close to. Help me find the right man, who You are already speaking to about mentoring someone. Lead me as I approach him and help us both to know our relationship is of You. Thank You for always leading me to a better place. I look forward to what you're going to do over the next days, weeks and years of my life.

Notes: *What did you hear God saying to you about finding a mentor?*

DAY 27

Philippians 3:12-14 - *Not that I have already obtained it or have already become perfect, but I press on so that I may lay hold of that for which also I was laid hold of by Christ Jesus. Brethren, I do not regard myself as having laid hold of it yet; but one thing I do: forgetting what lies behind and reaching forward to what lies ahead, I press on toward the goal for the prize of the upward call of God in Christ Jesus.*

Sometimes it feels like there is so much to do, and so much to remember, you can easily get under the pile of guilt, shame, regret and simply think — "what's the use, I can't do all this".

Here is a passage that gives all of us hope along our marriage/life journey. We all make mistakes. No one does it perfectly. How do you respond when you drop the ball?

Paul was a hater and persecutor of Christians. He was responsible for the deaths of many believers and the heartache of countless families — yet, God had a plan for his life - a plan that included his salvation. This plan also included using him to preach the gospel to unbelieving Gentiles, to pen multiple chapters of the Bible, and to become a pillar and hero of the Christian faith. How did Paul live with himself? How did he deal with the mental harassment, the guilt, the shame and the ball and chain from his past?

Here is how he did it, and here is how you can do it too. You too have baggage. You have a past or at least a closet you don't want to open, and you really don't want anyone else to open. Even if you have a rather plain vanilla past, compared to Paul and others, you have made, are making, and will make — mistakes. You have let God and other people down.

Despite your best efforts, you often fall short.

List two areas in your marriage where you know you often fall short.
1. _____
2. _____

Paul gives husbands two great pieces of advice: 1.) forget what lies behind. Ask God (and others if necessary) to forgive you, repent (change your ways), and get on with the mission God is leading you to; 2.) Reach forward – press forward – to what lies ahead. The windshield of your life should be much larger than the rearview mirror. God forgives. God restores. God gives second, third and fourth chances.

Why is it so hard to forget what lies behind? _____
_____
_____
_____

For the accuser of our brothers and sisters (Satan) has been thrown down to earth, the one who accuses them before our God day and night. ~ Revelation 12:10

I am convinced many husbands (and wives) don't forget the past because they simply don't want to. They sometimes use the past to get what they want today, or they may actually find comfort in being a victim of their past. I have met many people that can't move forward in life, because their poor self esteem compels them to seek "poor me" type sympathy and attention from others. They secretly need that attention and affirmation because they don't receive it elsewhere.

When you fall, why is it so hard to get back up again and eagerly press ahead? _____
_____
_____
_____

I have also found countless husband and wives (Christian people) who simply don't accept the fact that God has truly forgiven them and that He loves them personally, deeply and unconditionally. They listen to the enemy's lie that tells them they aren't good enough, or that their sin is too big or too dark

for God to forgive. They can't look ahead with hope because they can't receive the complete love and forgiveness of the Father, and trust that He has completely forgiven them, restored them, and will only lead them to better places.

If you have fallen for this lie, please read and meditate on Luke 15, beginning at verse eleven. Pay particular attention to the response of the father.

God still has a plan for you. He has called you to achieve much in His name. Don't let the enemy convince you otherwise. What would Christianity be today if people like Moses, David, Peter and Paul would have withered away into obscurity after disobeying and disappointing God? God creates all of us with a mission. Our life matters to God. It matters to your wife and children. It matters to His kingdom. Don't let failure or setback keep you down. Get up, dust yourself off, and get back in step with Jesus. Remember – God is a God of fresh starts. Get back in the race.

Crafted Prayer

Father, thank You that You love me. You forgive me and give me a reason to get back in the game of life. I have failed You and failed those who love me most. Help me live a deliberate life, sold out to You and what You want for me. I want to be clean before You and before my wife. Give me the courage to clean the slate with her, and to move forward with my eyes fixed on You. I want to be the husband You call me to be, and with Your help I can be.

Thank You for Your unconditional, extravagant love for me. I will never deserve it, but am so thankful for it. Help me to forget what lies behind me, and not let the enemy convince me that I am a victim. I am Your son and You love me. You have great plans for me and I can trust You. Thank You for a fresh start – today.

Notes: *What did you hear God saying to you about your past, and your future?*

_____
_____
_____
_____
_____
_____
_____

> **"You cannot control what happens to you, but you can control your attitude toward what happens to you."**
> **~ Brian Tracy**

DAY 28

Colossians 4:2 - *Devote yourselves to prayer, keeping alert in it with an attitude of thanksgiving;*

Romans 12:12 – *rejoicing in hope, persevering in tribulation, devoted to prayer*

Have you ever tried to make toast without plugging the toaster into the wall socket? Ever used a chain saw without ever starting it up? Power tools and appliances are designed to be used best when empowered from the appropriate power source. The same is true for you. Life functions about as well as an unplugged toaster if you don't ever access your source of power and strength.

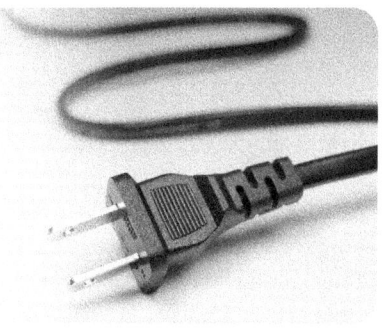

Prayer is your divine power cord to God. By accessing Him in conversation, you instantly tap into His unlimited resources of wisdom, patience, peace, love and power. He is the source of everything you need in this life. This is why scripture encourages you over and over to pray. In today's verses you are exhorted to devote yourself to prayer. There is a huge difference in occasional (when you get in trouble) prayer and being devoted/committed/dedicated to prayer.

So, what is prayer anyway? Most of us grew up learning a bedtime prayer and possibly hearing someone bless our food at mealtime. Other than that, we have little training in prayer.

Where and when did you learn how to pray? _____
_____

Prayer is actually a conversation with God. It is a dialogue, not a monologue. God desires to speak with you also. He actually wants to commune with you more than you want to commune with Him. He is always present, and always listening. He always hears and always cares. He is never unable to hear or answer your prayer. He may not answer it the way you would like (He may say "no", or "not now", or "not your way but mine" – but He always answers.

I Thessalonians 5 encourages you to "pray without ceasing". This would not be part of scripture if God was not listening "without ceasing" too. As a husband, you will make huge strides in your relationship with your wife if you will do two things that are so simple, but amazingly hard to do:

1. Spend large amounts of time in personal prayer/communion with God
2. Pray with your wife on a consistent basis

How much time do you spend in prayer on any given day?
_____

How often do you pray with your wife? _____

In order to have time to do either (much less both) of the above, you have to sacrifice time spent doing something else. That's where things get difficult. We like our television programs, our sleep, our hobbies and our "to-do" list. We never seem to have enough time to do the things that count most. Truth is – we <u>do</u> have time. The honest answer is – we just don't care or see the need in it. Things are going okay right now, so I'll just wait to pray until I have a crisis. <u>You will find time to do the things you really want to do, the things you find most valuable</u>.

"Prayerlessness is an insult to God. Every prayerless day is a statement by a helpless individual, 'I do not need God today'."
~ Ben Jennings

One of the fastest ways to experience significant growth as a Christian man is to spend more time in prayer with God. One of the fastest ways to experience greater oneness and intimacy with your wife is to spend time praying with her. In prayer she hears your heart and feels more emotionally and spiritually connected to you. She will experience your leadership and your vulnerability in prayer more than any other place. Don't miss out on what God has in store for your marriage by not taking time to pray with your wife (mealtime prayers don't count).

Name two things that stand in the way of you spending more time in prayer with God and with your wife? _____
_____
_____

Consistent prayer flows from a desperate heart. Until you fully realize that you are desperate without God's daily wisdom, strength, hope and leadership, you will never see the need to become devoted to prayer. Prayer moves the heart of God, and it stirs  the heart of your wife – like nothing else you can do, say or buy. This one thing will produce more significant change in you and in your marriage than all the books, cd's, seminars and classes combined.

Crafted Prayer

Father, here I am praying to You and asking You to help me pray. I desire to spend more time with You, but I am selfish and need You to do a work in my heart to want to sacrifice my comfort and pleasure in order to experience the amazing pleasure of knowing You better. Take my desire away for those things that keep me from You and give me a heart that longs for more time in Your presence.

Forgive me Lord, for not being more devoted to praying with my wife. She longs to know my heart and to experience my spiritual leadership in that way, and I have let her and You down. Show me where we can find time in our busy lives to get still together and experience Your presence together. I am desperate for You to do a work in me or it won't get done. I ask for these things believing that I will receive them, in Jesus' name.

Notes: *What did you hear God saying to you about becoming devoted to prayer?*

_____
_____
_____
_____
_____
_____
_____
_____
_____
_____
_____
_____
_____
_____

Draw near to God, and he will draw near to you.
~ James 4:8

DAY 29

James 1:22-24 - But prove yourselves doers of the word, and not merely hearers who delude themselves. For if anyone is a hearer of the word and not a doer, he is like a man who looks at his natural face in a mirror; for once he has looked at himself and gone away, he has immediately forgotten what kind of person he was.

James 13:17 - Now that you know these things, God will bless you for doing them.

Philippians 2:13 - for it is God who is at work in you, both to will and to do His good pleasure.

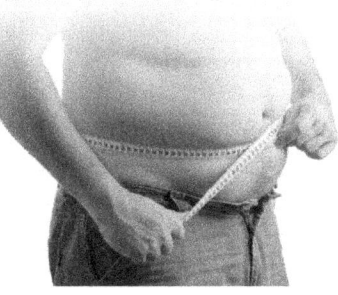

Gary Gilmore, the notorious spree-killer, uttered the words "Let's do it" just before a firing squad executed him in Utah in 1977. Years later, the phrase became the inspiration for Nike's famous "Just Do It" sports apparel campaign. The thought by Nike was basically to "stop thinking about exercising; stop talking about it; just go do it". Exercise won't happen until your body starts moving.

As I told you before you started this Challenge, nothing is going to change in your life or in your marriage if all you do is read this book and fill in the blanks. Even if you are sincere about wanting to change, nothing will happen until you make the conscious decision to "do something"…… and then start doing it.

These verses from James are reminders that: 1) you deceive yourself if you never do what you know is the right thing to do, and 2) God will bless you if you begin doing them. The choice, as always, is yours to make. Do you really want to experience change in your walk with God and in your relationship with your wife? If the real answer is "yes", then you will have to make the hard choices involved in putting the truths found in this Challenge into practice in your life. There is no better time than now. No one, not even God, can do it for you. He will rush to help you, but you must start doing.

What would honestly keep you from deciding to live your life as a doer of His Word and not a hearer only? _____

_____

What do you think your wife's response would be if she saw you making the effort to live your life and your marriage based on God's Word? _____

_____

Now, there are a few of you who have gotten this far in the Challenge, and are honestly saying to yourself, "I'm not sure I really want to do all this", "this sounds like a lot of work". Maybe you want the results, but aren't sure you have the will to do what it takes to achieve them. That's why the verse from Philippians 2:13 is included above.

God is so big. He is so amazing. He is so loving that He promises to even give you the will (the "want to") and the ability to do His will. How cool is that? If you ask Him, He will do a work in your heart to change your will. Once you see that happening, He will also give you the ability to "do" what He is calling you to do.

Today you have more books, classes and seminars on marriage than ever before in history. You have probably heard many sermons, and have read many scriptures about marriage and how to treat your wife. If knowing was enough, American Christians should have the lowest divorce rate of all married groups – but they are still running the same percentage (51%) as those who claim to have no faith at all. Knowledge alone will not change your heart, or your will. Change will not happen just because you attend a class or seminar, or read a great book on marriage.

What couples need today is not more information, but transformation. ~ Rob Thorpe

Change will only happen as you make conscious choices each and every day to live as a deliberate follower of Christ, and a deliberate husband. Review Days 12 and 13 again in light of the last few days, and reevaluate your desire to change things in your life. Take the time to get alone with God and ask Him for direction and courage.

What is one major thing you know you need to change in your life in order to transform your walk with Christ? _____
_____

What is one major thing you know you need to change in your life in order to transform your relationship with your wife?
_____
_____
_____

Starting is always the hardest part of the process. Whether you want to lose a few pounds, or stop smoking, or conquer a bad habit – or transform your life – the most difficult steps are the first ones. They typically don't feel good, and your flesh screams at you to forget it. If you're really serious this time – just do it! God says in our second verse today that He will bless you if you do. Wouldn't you like to feel God's blessing on your life, and on your marriage?

Crafted Prayer

Father, the Challenge is almost over, but my transformation is just beginning. Today I choose to say "yes" to You and to the things You desire for me. I want to be a doer and not just a hearer. My good intentions are not enough. I need Your supernatural power and blessing if I am ever to become the man and the husband You desire me to be. My wife and family deserve it, but more importantly, You deserve it. You gave everything for me, and I have given little. Forgive my apathy and selfish focus.

I need You to overcome the selfish inertia in my life and to help me break free from the "life's about me" mentality that draws me like a magnet. Set me free Lord, by the power of Your Spirit. Energize me to get started on an amazing adventure with You like I have never experienced before. Speak to me. Strengthen me. Lead me. I yield my life and my marriage to You. Make me the best husband on the planet, as I abide in You. Thank You Lord.

Notes: *What did you hear God saying to you about being a doer of His Word?*

_____
_____
_____
_____
_____
_____
_____
_____

DAY 30

Matthew 4:19 - *"Come, follow me," Jesus said, "and I will make you fishers of men."*

Remember, Jesus told his disciples to follow Him and He would be responsible to make them fishers of men. He didn't say "learn a lot of stuff, study hard, be good boys, go to church and read your Bible, and you will become fishers of men". Jesus only asked them to do one thing - follow Him.

Following someone in Jesus' day meant you left everything and literally walked with them every day and every night. You spent all of your time with them. You learned from them, asked them questions, listened for answers and witnessed their life 24/7. Christ followers began to be called "Christians" or "little Christ's".

Somewhere along the way being a Christian, or Christ-follower, has digressed to the point that anyone who has said a prayer of salvation, or goes to church and believes in God feels completely comfortable using the term Christian. I am convinced many people have asked Jesus into their hearts as Savior, but have little or no intention of having Him rule as Lord/Master/King of their personal, daily lives.

What about you? Would you say that Christ is currently the Lord of your life and everything in it?

What would your life look like if that were true? _____
_____
_____

You are created to live life with Jesus. As John Eldredge puts it in his book *Walking with God* – "It is our deepest need as human beings, to learn to live intimately with God. It is what we were made for." To know Christ personally and intimately is what being a follower, or Christian, is supposed to be about.

The cry of Paul's heart as he wrote to the church at Philippi, was "that I might know Him". Paul knew of Jesus, and had even experienced an amazing encounter with Him at his salvation – but he longed to really "know" Him deeply and intimately. Jesus told us that we would know Him because the Spirit would live inside us. He has given us the ability to truly know Him – if we choose to.

Enjoying a real, and meaningful relationship with anyone - wife, child, friend, etc. - takes time. Time together with that person is crucial in developing a lasting and meaningful bond. Are you honestly putting in the time and energy it takes to spend that kind of time with Jesus? Do you deliberately "leave your nets and follow him" every day of your life, or do you rush through a quick devotional and go on about your life?

Today - what is one choice you can make in your life and in your schedule to allow yourself more time with Jesus? _____
_____
_____

This 30-Day Challenge has been designed to expose you to crucial verses of Scripture that call you to a deeper walk with Christ and a deeper devotion and appreciation for your wife. We started with this truth, and now we sum the entire Challenge up with the same phrase – "Follow me, and I will make you…"

The responsibility to follow is yours. The responsibility to "make you" into the man and husband you desire to be, is Christ's. It sounds pretty simple, but you know it's not. Following takes effort. It takes a deliberate choice every morning of your life, not to have a "quiet time", but to commune and fellowship with the amazing King of Kings.

To be a follower assumes someone else is leading. You have to lay down your right to lead your life, your way, and voluntarily give Jesus the car keys. You have to humble yourself and reach that place where you know you are desperate without Him. You also have to know deep in your soul that you are a precious son of His, your life (every detail of it) matters to Him, and that you are 100%, unconditionally forgiven for your past and free from all the guilt and shame associated with it.

God is a Father you can trust. He has "good plans for you", and has promised to do "exceedingly abundantly above all that you can ask or think" if you will just go and trust Him. I pray that you won't miss another day of walking with your King. **Follow Him, and He will make you...............**

Crafted Prayer

Father, thank You that You love me and have great plans for my life. Help me to trust You more. Help me to surrender my life daily to Your will and direction for me. Give me the faith to let go of the things I think I control about my life and give them freely into Your hands. I want to be fully devoted to You. Make me a new man, a new husband, and start today, Lord.

I also want to be fully devoted to my wife and to our marriage. I ask that You do a deep and lasting work in my heart to more fully appreciate, encourage, honor and love her as You command me to. I need Your strength, Your wisdom and Your patience to love her as You love the church. Speak to me today, and every day from here on, about how I can show her my love, and honor her as Your precious gift to me. Give me the words to speak to her, and help my actions show her that I am devoted to her for a lifetime. Show us both how we can honor You in our marriage and bring You glory as we journey together toward oneness.

Notes: *God is speaking to you right now. What do you hear Him saying?*

_____
_____
_____
_____
_____
_____

> **"My sheep hear My voice, and I know them, and they follow Me"** –Jesus–
> ~ John 10:27

HUSBAND RESOURCES

Need Prayer?
Need Encouragement?
Need a Mentor?

Contact MK at marriagesthatmatter@gmail.com

Visit the blog designed for husbands and written by husbands: www.husband.wordpress.com

Want to host a MarriageKeepers Seminar at your church, or schedule Rob Thorpe as a speaker at your men's, couples, or church retreat or conference?

Contact MK at marriagesthatmatter@gmail.com

To order additional copies of Husband - A User's Guide: reNEWed, the 30-day Challenge or The Quiet Time Myth, visit - www.marriagekeepers.org, or email us at marriagesthatmatter@gmail.com

> **Dear children (husbands), let us not love with words or tongue, but with actions and in truth.**
> **~ 1 John 3:18**

www.ingramcontent.com/pod-product-compliance
Lightning Source LLC
Chambersburg PA
CBHW071709040426
42446CB00011B/1989